James Aitchison

The cross of Christ as set forth in the Apostolic writings

James Aitchison

The cross of Christ as set forth in the Apostolic writings

ISBN/EAN: 9783337257415

Printed in Europe, USA, Canada, Australia, Japan

Cover: Foto ©Lupo / pixelio.de

More available books at **www.hansebooks.com**

THE
CROSS OF CHRIST

AS SET FORTH IN THE APOSTOLIC WRITINGS

BY

JAMES AITCHISON

Minister of Erskine Church Falkirk

AUTHOR OF "SIGNA CHRISTI" "THE CHRONICLE OF MITES"
"A BAG WITH HOLES" ETC

———✦———

FALKIRK
JOHN CALLANDER
1896

[ALL RIGHTS RESERVED]

TO
THE SESSION AND CONGREGATION
OF
ERSKINE CHURCH, FALKIRK,
THIS BOOK
ON THE MAIN THEME
OF A TWENTY-ONE YEARS' MINISTRY
IS VERY AFFECTIONATELY
INSCRIBED.

PREFACE.

THE following discourses on the Cross of Christ were delivered in Erskine Church, Falkirk, during the months of December, January, and February, 1895-96. Some who heard them expressed a desire for their publication. The request of friends can seldom be regarded as a sufficient reason for adopting this course; but, as during the period they were being preached, the author reached what might be called his "majority" as a minister, he thought he might venture to print them for private circulation, as a kind of memorial of his twenty-one years' service of the congregation in the gospel of Christ. On this account also he has added a sermon delivered on the twenty-first anniversary of his ministry. The number of those beyond the circle of the congregation who indicated a desire to possess copies has somewhat enlarged the scope of the intended circulation, and compelled wider publication than was at first designed.

The discourses are printed *verbatim* as they were delivered, with the addition of some notes and the Scripture references. The study is one which has proved interesting and stimulating to the author, and the principle he has adopted in pursuing it is that so happily expressed in the wise words of Thomas Fuller, " Diamonds only can cut diamonds : and no such comment on Scripture as the Scripture." The usual commentaries have been consulted, but reliance has been chiefly placed on the self-interpreting power of the Word of God. In most instances of quotation from the Old and New Testaments the renderings of the Revised Version have been given, though to this there are some exceptions, when those of the Authorised Version seemed preferable. A short Appendix has been added in vindication of the point of view which has been adopted in this study.

The author desires to express his cordial thanks to the Rev. John Campbell, St Margaret's Church, Dunfermline, who kindly read the proof sheets, and verified the references, as also to Hugh Campbell, Esq., LL.D., High School, Falkirk, who rendered timely and valuable service of a like nature.

The Book is sent forth with the earnest prayer that it may prove, through the gracious agency of the Holy Spirit, a means for the confirmation of some in the faith, and for the leading of others into the experience of the soul-healing and soul-sanctifying power of the Cross of Christ.

Falkirk, August, 1896.

CONTENTS.

PREFACE . . . . V.

THE CROSS OF CHRIST.

I. Obedient unto Death:
"Became obedient unto death, even the death of the Cross." Philippians ii. 8. 9

II. The Joy Set before Him:
"Who for the joy that was set before Him endured the Cross, despising the shame." Hebrews xii. 2. 27

III. Peace Through the Blood:
"Having made peace through the blood of His Cross." Colossians i. 20. 45

IV. Reconciliation by the Cross:
"That He might reconcile both unto God in one body by the Cross, having slain the enmity thereby." Ephesians ii. 16. 63

V. Triumphing in the Cross:
"Blotting out the handwriting of ordinances, that was against us, which was contrary to us, and took it out of the way, nailing it to His Cross: and having spoiled principalities and powers, He made a shew of them openly, triumphing over them in it." Colossians ii. 14, 15. 81

VI. Preaching the Cross—Foolishness and Power:
"For the preaching of the Cross is to them that perish foolishness: but unto us which are saved it is the power of God." 1 Corinthians i. 18. 101

viii.   THE CROSS OF CHRIST.

VII. MAKING VOID THE CROSS:

"To preach the Gospel, not with wisdom of words, lest the Cross of Christ should be made of none effect." 1 Corinthians i. 17. . . 119

VIII. THE OFFENCE OF THE CROSS:

"The Offence of the Cross." Galatians v. 11. . . 137

IX. THE ENEMIES OF THE CROSS:

"The Enemies of the Cross of Christ." Philippians iii. 18. 155

X. PERSECUTION FOR THE CROSS:

"Suffer persecution for the Cross of Christ." Galatians vi. 12. 173

XI. GLORYING IN THE CROSS:

"God forbid that I should glory, save in the Cross of our Lord Jesus Christ." Galatians vi. 14. 191

THE PREACHER'S IDEAL.

"I have not shunned to declare unto you all the counsel of God." Acts xx. 27. 211

APPENDIX.

THE MIND OF CHRIST. 229

I.
OBEDIENT UNTO DEATH.

*'Twas thus He suffered, though a Son,
  Foreknowing, choosing, feeling all,
Until the perfect work was done,
  And drunk the bitter cup of gall.*--CONDER

THE CROSS OF CHRIST.

I.—OBEDIENT UNTO DEATH.

Philippians II. 8—"*Became obedient unto death, even the death of the Cross.*"

I PROPOSE to give a series of discourses on the Cross of Christ. In one sense, all evangelical presentations of the truth that set forth Jesus Christ and Him crucified as the means of salvation, may be termed discourses on the Cross of Christ, but it is with a much more specific meaning that I now make use of this phrase as descriptive of the line of thought and investigation which I desire in this and succeeding expositions to pursue. For I propose entirely to confine our considerations to those passages in which the word "cross" occurs, and to seek to set before you such spiritual truths, relative to the sufferings of our Lord, as they may be found to contain. We shall discover that there is very considerable variety in the phases or aspects of verity that are thus presented, and that the enquiry will, whilst constantly bringing us into contact with the gospel of Christ, place that gospel before us from many widely different and exceedingly interesting and instructive points of view. And I earnestly trust that, as Sabbath after Sabbath our gaze is again and again fixed on the great fact of the dying of the Lord Jesus, and, as we behold that scene from many and varied standpoints, the Cross will become more precious to us as the symbol of salvation; that those who have never beheld it in faith may be enabled so to see it; and that those who already rely upon it, may find its attraction grow upon them, and its sacred influence increase, until they be constrained to say like the apostle, "God forbid that I should glory, save in the Cross of our Lord Jesus Christ."[1]

The instances in which the term "cross" is used in the New Testament are not so many as we would antecedently imagine. Apart from the gospels, I have only found eleven passages in which the word occurs, and, with one exception, these passages are in the Epistles of Paul—that exception being in the Epistle to the Hebrews, which some think was also written by Paul's hand. One remarkable thing is that our Lord is not recorded as having ever named the instrument of His death. The word "cross" He did indeed use, but on all occasions as applying to that which those were required to endure who wished to become His followers. He said, for instance, "If any man would come after Me, let him deny himself, and take up his cross and follow Me,"[2] and again "He that doth not take his cross and follow after Me, is not worthy of Me."[3] In this, and in all similar cases, it will be observed that He is employing the term figuratively, though as may be well imagined not without reference to what was to be His own experience. That He never calls the instrument of His death by its name was not due to ignorance on His part of the manner in which He was to meet His fate. The Cross was before Him from the very first. There is a striking picture of Holman Hunt, entitled "The Shadow of the Cross." The scene is the interior of the

[1] Gal. vi. 14. [2] Mat. xvi. 24. [3] Mat. x. 38.

OBEDIENT UNTO DEATH. 13

carpenter's workshop at Nazareth, and the figures in it are Jesus the young Carpenter and His mother. It is evening, and the last rays of the setting sun are flooding the room, and falling upon the wall behind. The weary Workman has raised Himself up from His day's heavy toil, and is stretching out His arms in order to relax His jaded limbs, and the startled mother sees on the wall at the back the shadow of her Son's extended form as if fixed upon the Cross, a sight that, though it be but a shadow, sends already the sword through her heart. As in this picture, so seems it to have been with the language of Christ in reference to His death. The Cross He never names, but the shadow of it we often see. Even at the very beginning of His ministry He said "As Moses lifted up the serpent in the wilderness even so must the Son of Man be lifted up,"[4] and once again near its close He recurs to this lifting up and predicts its wondrous effect.[5] Then although He names not the Cross He does not hesitate to say the Son of Man must be crucified,[6] thus bringing before the eyes of His disciples the very image of that dread engine of suffering and death, which was no doubt as repugnant to their minds as it was abhorrent to their frames.

Another point to be noted is that the Evangelists in their records never mention the Cross with a doctrinal signification, that is, do not in any place speak of it in the sense in which Paul speaks of it, or in the sense in which we refer to it in the present day—viz., as the centre of the great verity of the gospel. All their references to it are purely historical. John tells us that Jesus went forth from the place of judgment "bearing His Cross"[7]; Matthew, Mark, and Luke record

[4] John iii. 14. [5] John xii. 32. [6] Mat. xx. 18, 19. [7] John xix. 17.

how the soldiers afterwards laid it on the shoulders of Simon the Cyrenian to carry after Jesus;[8] the two former also tell us of the taunt of the priests and Pharisees who invited Jesus, if He were really the Christ, to come down from the Cross and save Himself;[9] in the fourth gospel we are informed that Pilate wrote a title and put it above the Cross,[10] "JESUS OF NAZARETH, THE KING OF THE JEWS"; once more the same narrative records how there stood by the Cross of Jesus His mother, and other women,[11] and lastly in this account we are told that the Jews were anxious that the body should not remain on the Cross on the Sabbath day.[12] Now, as will be observed, every one of these notices is of an historical nature; we are not directly brought into contact with any specific Christian truth by means of them—we may draw spiritual inferences from their suggestive statements and their surroundings, but they were not penned by the evangelists with the avowed or evident intention of setting forth any special verity of the gospel of Christ. They are simply the necessary incidental references in the narrative by which the facts are clearly placed before our minds.

It is, however, altogether different when we turn from the Gospel to the Epistles. The term "Cross" has become a word of deep spiritual import—the thing itself has become a symbol of profound gospel truth. And so there is not a passage in which it is used that is not full of intense significance, and that may not most profitably be made the theme of special inquiry and meditation. As I have said, these passages are not numerous, being only eleven in number; but

[8] Mat. xxvii. 32; Mark xv. 21; Luke xxiii. 26.
[9] Mat. xxvii. 41-43; Mark xv. 31, 32.   [10] John xix. 19.
[11] John xix. 25.   [12] John xix. 31.

OBEDIENT UNTO DEATH.

they are of the very greatest import. They may be divided into groups which might be thus characterised :—

1st. The spirit in which Christ suffered; and this is set forth in the passage before us, "Became obedient unto death, even the death of the Cross," as also in the Epistle to the Hebrews, "Who for the joy that was set before Him, endured the Cross, despising the shame."[13]

2nd. The purpose for which Christ suffered; He "made peace through the blood of His Cross,"[14] He "reconciled both unto God in one body by the Cross,"[15] and as for the accusation against us He "took it out of the way, nailing it to His Cross."[16]

3rd. The effect of Christ's suffering; "The preaching of the Cross is to them that perish foolishness; but unto us which are saved it is the power of God."[17]

4th. The obstacles to the legitimate effect of Christ's sufferings; the "wisdom of words" that make "void" "the Cross of Christ,"[18] "the offence of the Cross,"[19] and "the enemies of the Cross of Christ."[20]

5th. The co-suffering of disciples with Christ—viz., "to suffer persecution for the Cross of Christ,"[21] and then lastly

6th. We have the triumph of the disciple in and through the suffering of his Lord, "God forbid that I should glory, save in the Cross of our Lord Jesus Christ, by whom the world is crucified unto me, and I unto the world."[22] These then are the themes that are to come before us in this study; some of them I have touched upon in the past—it is impossible that I should have preached to you the gospel so long and

---

[13] Heb. xii. 2.   [14] Col. i. 20.   [15] Eph. ii. 16.
[16] Col. ii. 14.   [17] I. Cor. i. 18.   [18] I. Cor. i. 17.
[19] Gal. v. 11.   [20] Phil. iii. 18.   [21] Gal. vi. 12.   [22] Gal. vi. 14.

not have more or less directly dealt with such topics—but all of them we may now view in a fresh light, and we shall find that they cast upon each other gleams of lustre, so that we better apprehend them as a great and glowing cluster than as separate gems.

The text which I have chosen this afternoon comes naturally as the first of the series. It is the link between the merely historical references to the Cross, which we find in the evangelists, and the doctrinal notices which meet us in the Epistles. For, as you will observe, it partakes of the character both of the one and of the other. It records that Jesus suffered the death of the Cross, but records it as an act of supreme obedience. And it moreover sets forth this as the last and most important step in a descending development that seems to range from the highest to the lowest possible position. For there is placed before us, in the preceding part of the passage, a series of humiliations passed through by our Lord, which lead us from co-equality with God to degradation the most profound with man. The path of this downward career actually stretches over the entire diameter of the moral universe, beginning on the loftiest plane of spiritual eminence and ending in the death of One who is treated as a malefactor. To estimate the difference between the first and the last of it we require to measure the distance between the Throne of the Eternal and the Cross of the Condemned.

But it is only to the final phase of this humiliation that our attention is turned to-day, for we confine our thoughts to the statement that our Lord "became obedient unto death, even the death of the Cross." And in respect of this statement looked at from the point of view which we are now occupying I propose to speak briefly of three matters, viz.:—

    1st. The Cross as an instrument of death;

    2nd. Christ's death on the Cross as the crown of His obedience; and

    3rd. Why the Cross, instead of other possible modes of death and sacrifice?

First, then, let us consider *the Cross as an instrument of death.* Its simplest form, as has been pointed out, consists of two pieces of wood, one standing erect, the other crossing it at right angles, and in this form it has been known as an instrument of punishment from the earliest ages. In all likelihood its shape was suggested by trees and their stretched-out branches. To be suspended from a tree and to be crucified were considered punishments of virtually the same import, according to Cicero, whilst Seneca describes the Cross by a phrase which may be freely translated, "the accursed tree." As a mode of exacting the last penalty of the law it, or a like instrument, was in use amongst the Scythians, the Persians, the Carthaginians, the Greeks, the Romans, the ancient Germans, and other nations of antiquity. Indeed there is reason to believe that in one form or another it has been employed more or less by the majority of peoples of olden times, and even traces of it have been found amongst the Chinese.

But there is another point of very considerable interest in regard to this to which it is fitting here to draw your attention. The sign of the Cross is found as a sacred symbol amongst many nations of early times. On this account one of the Latin fathers of the Church—Tertullian—called these peoples, *crucis religiosos*, that is, devotees of the Cross. Other writers tell us that by the Indians and the Egyptians the form was employed as a holy sign, and may be seen still in stones cut with hieroglyphics and cuneiform inscriptions. It "is generally understood to be symbolical of the divinity or eternal life." That it was more than a mere ornament seems to be indicated by the fact that when Theodosius, the Christian Roman Emperor, along with his victorious army had over-run and reduced the valley of the Nile, the Egyptian priests sought to save the temple of Serapis from destruction, by pointing to the crosses on its walls as setting forth something in common between their religion and the Christian faith. There is indeed abundant proof that, for some reason or another, the Cross was not merely an instrument of punishment, but had attached to it a sacred significance even before the crucifixion of our Lord for ever sanctified it in the eyes of men. [23]

But at the same time we must remember that at the time of Christ it was both the most cruel and the most degrading of all modes of execution. It was reserved for the death of the malefactor and the slave. It was regarded as stamping with everlasting infamy those who suffered upon it; it attached a stigma to them which nothing whatever could remove. And this was probably the reason why the Jewish enemies of our Lord were so eager that He should suffer it. Pilate gave them the opportunity of putting Him to death by their own law—that was by the process of stoning, but they rejected it. [24] They realised that, if He were merely stoned, He might take rank with other martyrs of the Jewish nation,

---

[23] See Geikie's *Life and Words of Christ*, Cap. lxiii.; Farrar's *Life of Christ*, Cap. lxi.; Article *Cross*, *Encyclopædia Brittanica*.
[24] John xviii. 31. 32.

who were even then held in high veneration, and who had suffered this fate. But they never conceived it possible that He could be crucified and thereafter be held in reverence by any of the human race; they thought He must of necessity be for ever execrated, that His followers would become ashamed of Him, and that no one would have the hardihood to proclaim himself or herself a disciple of One who had died so shameful a death. Let us keep these three points in view then, regarding the Cross as an instrument of death, for they will help us in a further stage of our considerations—1st, It was a universal mode of punishment; 2nd, The sign of it was used as a holy symbol; and 3rd, It was a mode of death the most infamous that was ever contrived by man.

But now let us consider in the second place here, *Christ's death on the Cross as the crown of His obedience.* This is indeed the main theme before us, but it is most closely connected with the other points which at this stage fall to be noted. He " became obedient unto death, even the death of the Cross." The question is, To whom did He become obedient? and on the answer to this question the whole of the significance of the Cross depends. It was not to man. It does not mean that He submitted without murmuring to what wicked hands contrived against Him. As a matter of fact He did so submit—He gave His back to the smiters, and His cheeks to them that plucked off the hair.[25] He made no resistance, but " as a lamb that was led to the slaughter, and as a sheep before her shearers is dumb, yea He opened not His mouth."[26] But this is not the fact which is emphasised in our text—it is a far other and more momentous

[25] Isa. l. 6.   [26] Isa. liii. 7.

feature that the words we are considering bring before us.

I note further that it is not that He submitted Himself to the enemy of mankind; that He let Satan have his will of Him, and wreak out his vengeance upon Him. No doubt the Devil was at the root of the evil that was done against our Lord; the gospel tells us that it was the Devil that put the traitorous purpose into the heart of Judas Iscariot, [27] and no doubt he had a hand in all the rest. But Jesus in no way submitted to Satan. He said "The Prince of this world cometh and hath nothing in Me," [28] a statement which, if we understand it rightly, excludes all possibility of our thinking, even for a moment, that the words before us have any reference to the relation of the Saviour to the great Adversary.

There is indeed but one possible meaning. The motto of Christ's mission to the world is surely contained in these words—words which, in various sayings of His, Jesus virtually appropriated to Himself—"Lo, I am come; in the roll of the Book it is written of Me: I delight to do Thy will, O My God; yea, Thy law is within My heart." [29] It is obedience to the Father that is spoken of in our text. It was the Father's will that He should suffer death, even the death of the Cross. Does not Christ himself say "Therefore doth the Father love Me, because I lay down My life." [30] This Cross then had been in the counsels of eternity. It was the appointed way of death for our Redeemer, the mode pre-determined upon even whilst the Son sat on the throne of co-equality with the Father. It was the goal before the Son when, as recounted in the passage of which our text forms part, He thought not his equality with God a thing to be

[27] John xiii. 2. [28] John xiv. 30. [29] Ps. xl. 7. [30] John x. 17.

grasped at and retained, and so stepped down from His high eminence and began that course which is traced in the words that follow: He "emptied Himself, taking the form of a servant, being made in the likeness of men; and being found in fashion as a man, He humbled Himself, becoming obedient *even* unto death, yea, the death of the Cross." Now into all the mystery of this antecedent devoting of the Divine Victim to such a fate we have not time at present to enter. It will come before us in connection with other phases of the Cross which we are in this course to consider, and we may meanwhile leave it with the remark that we shall find that it equally illustrates the wisdom and the love of God, and that it may well bring to our lips the exclamation of the apostle, "O the depth of the riches both of the wisdom and the knowledge of God! how unsearchable are His judgments, and His ways past tracing out [31]!"

We must now in conclusion address ourselves to the question, to which we are naturally led by the course of our considerations, *Why the Cross, instead of other possible modes of death and sacrifice?* It seems to me that the Cross, and the Cross alone, was the determined mode by which Christ was to suffer. He was not merely appointed to death—He was appointed to the Cross. It was not a matter of indifference what kind of death He should die; this manner of it was specially singled out and decreed. Now the ordinary answer to the question which I have proposed is that it was a death of special degradation, and therefore formed a fitting climax to the humiliation of Christ. There is, no doubt, this element in it, and it is a most important element in the view which

---

[31] Rom. xi. 33.

our text constrains us to take of it. But I do not feel that it is an answer beyond which we may not in many particulars go. For there are other reasons—reasons suggested by the thoughts that have been already before us, and reasons arising from other considerations which may be quite legitimately and fittingly presented.

For example, we have seen that this was a universal mode of punishment—it was not like the stoning of the Jews or the poisoning of the Greeks, or the strangling of the Persians, or the beheading of the Scythians, merely a sectional or national mode of putting to death. And is it too much to suppose that He who was to die for all should die by the mode of putting to death that was most widely prevalent amongst the human race—the death that would accordingly be most widely understood as carrying with it a penal character, as being a death inflicted for transgression, and therefore as having the aspect of punishment inscribed upon its very face? It was the kind of death that would lead the greatest number of men to ask, What was the crime that led to its infliction? and that would accordingly most readily lead the greatest number into the discovery "He was wounded for our transgressions, He was bruised for our iniquities; the chastisement of our peace was upon Him; and with His stripes we are healed. All we like sheep have gone astray . . . and the Lord hath laid on Him the iniquity of us all." [32] Yes, it was surely befitting that He who was to be the universal Saviour, through His suffering, should die after the universal form of inflicting the last penalty of the law.

[32] Isa. liii. 5, 6.

But yet again, is there not something to be concluded from the fact that the form of this death was so widely used as a sign of highest and most sacred truth? Is there not in the double meaning thus existing in reference to it a kind of presage of that twofold aspect which attaches to the death of our Redeemer? On the Cross behold sin and holiness, glory and shame, majesty and meanness, strength and weakness, brought side by side, and coalescing in the person of Him who suffers there—the sin on Him and for which He dies, the holiness in Him and which carries the power of an endless life: the glory of His self-sacrifice, and the shame of His degrading death; His majesty as the Conqueror who there spoils principalities and powers, and the meanness of His aspect as the Man of Sorrows and acquainted with grief; and finally His strength as the Redeemer and Avenger, and His weakness as the Victim who bows His head and yields to death. Only on the Cross could such contrasts, so full of significance, be fully set forth, and in all their rich spiritual significance be exemplified.

On this, however, we cannot linger, for there are other reasons for the Cross that may be adduced, and must by no means be left out of account. As our Lord Himself in the very beginning of His ministry signified, His death must be like the elevation of the serpent in the wilderness a lifting up.[33] And the aim of this lifting up we are not left to conjecture, for He says regarding it, "and I, if I be lifted up from the earth will draw all men unto Me."[34] His Saviourhood must be exhibited before the eyes of all men, that His word of invitation may be interpreted to every soul, "Look unto

[33] John iii. 14. [34] John xii. 32.

Me, and be ye saved, all the ends of the earth." [35] There must be the opportunity through all time of man looking upon Him whom he has pierced: [36] opportunity for that repenting mourning that ever precedes the personal apprehension of salvation: opportunity for the rendering of the recompense to the Redeemer which His dying love merits, and which His suffering is set forth as ultimately producing, "He shall see of the travail of His soul, and shall be satisfied." [37]

For in other senses is the Cross as well a lifting up of the Lord. It is a lifting up not only that men may see, but that the Sufferer may be supremely exalted. It is a lifting up, that the glory of the thorn-crowned Head may be completed, and that the blood-drops on the temples of the Crucified One may shine as gems of the purest lustre through time and in eternity. It is a lifting up, that before the entire universe the ineffable grandeur of divine love may flash forth and bring to Him who displays it ascriptions of honour and glory and blessing. It is a lifting up, that through the spear-pierced wound we may see and adore the heart broken by its outraged affection for us, and that in the out-stretched arms we may have ever before us a symbol of the all-comprehensiveness of that yearning for the children of men, that would fain clasp them to the bleeding breast and hide them in the wounded side. All this and much more we might illustrate did our time permit; as it is we can only hint at these reasons for the Cross as the appointed mode of our Redeemer's death. Opportunity may present itself, whilst we consider the other passages that are to be before us, of

[35] Isa. xlv. 22   [36] Zech. xii. 10.   [37] Isa. liii. 11.

recurring to them. In the meantime is not the practical lesson of our present study sufficiently plain? Christ is lifted up on the Cross that you and I may accept Him as Saviour and adore Him as Lord. He bears the Cross that the Cross may not bear us. Let not His dying love, appearing in this most striking and suggestive form, be in vain for any of us. Let His obedience unto death, even the death of the Cross, constrain our obedience unto life, even the life that inherits the Throne.

> "Lord Jesu, when we stand afar
>   And gaze upon Thy holy Cross,
> In love of Thee and scorn of self,
>   Oh, may we count the world as loss!
>
> When we behold Thy bleeding wounds,
>   And the rough way that Thou hast trod,
> Make us to hate the load of sin
>   That lay so heavy on our God.
>
> O holy Lord! uplifted high
>   With outstretched arms, in mortal woe,
> Embracing in Thy wondrous love
>   The sinful world that lies below!
>
> Give us an ever-living faith
>   To gaze beyond the things we see;
> And in the mystery of Thy death
>   Draw us and all men unto Thee." [38]

[38] William Walsham How.

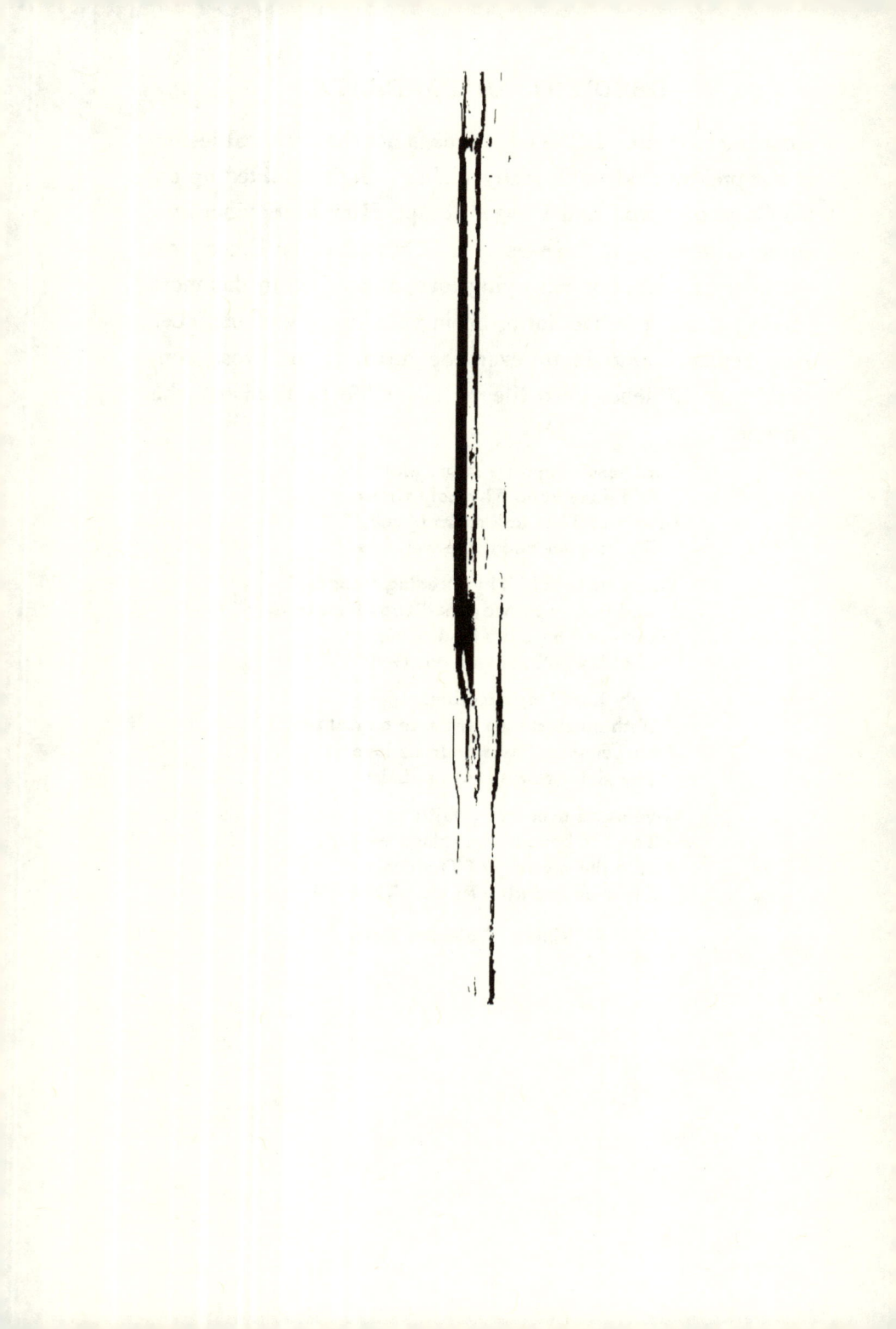

II.
THE JOY SET BEFORE HIM.

He shall see of the travail of His soul and shall be satisfied.—
ISAIAH LIII. 11.

Cling to His Cross; and let thy ceaseless prayer
  Be, that thy grasp may fail not! and, erelong,
Thou shalt ascend to that fair temple, where
  In strains ecstatic an innumerous throng
Of saints and seraphs, round the throne above,
  Proclaim for evermore that God is Love!

—THOMAS DAVIS.

THE CROSS OF CHRIST.

II.—THE JOY SET BEFORE HIM.

Hebrews XII. 2.—"Who for the joy that was set before Him, endured the Cross, despising the shame."

In these words we have the second of two statements to which I made reference in the discourse of last Sabbath afternoon as exhibiting the spirit in which Christ suffered on the Cross at Calvary. The first of these statements—"became obedient unto death, even the death of the Cross"—has already occupied our attention, and now we turn to what is practically the same theme, but looked at from a different point of view. The consideration of His becoming obedient unto death led us backward to the antecedents of Christ's suffering, whilst our contemplation of His enduring for the joy that was set before Him will lead us forward to its consequences. The Cross was both an end and a beginning—the end of a course of humiliation, the beginning of a course of exaltation, the end of a career of suffering, the beginning of an experience of felicity, the end of a self-renouncing servitude, the beginning of a self-asserting mastery. These contrasts show forth the difference between the standpoint which we occupied in last discourse and that which we must assume in this. For whereas in the former we had of necessity to go back to the preceding glory and honour of Christ in His position of co-equality with the Father on the heavenly throne—from which throne He descended by a downwardly sloping path to the very depths of the Cross—now, on the contrary, we must go forward to the succeeding glory and honour of Christ in the position of resumed co-equality with the Father on the heavenly throne—to which throne he ascends by a path that starts in the darkness of Calvary, and reaches its goal in that lustrous scene in which angels and redeemed shall offer the incense of perfected praise, and shall sing the song of loftiest adoration, " Worthy is the Lamb that hath been slain to receive the power, and riches, and wisdom, and might, and honour, and glory, and blessing." [1] This is the issue to which the passage to-day before us inevitably conducts.

You will observe that that passage occurs quite incidentally in the midst of an exhortation to faith and patience addressed to the readers of the Epistle to the Hebrews. That exhortation first sets forth the " great cloud of witnesses," presented in the martyr roll of the previous chapter, as an incitement to believers to pursue their course with fidelity, renunciation, and self-denial, and then concentrates the gaze of Christian disciples on Him who is at once the Goal and the Example of persevering spiritual life : " Looking unto Jesus the Author and Perfecter of our faith, who for the joy that was set before Him endured the Cross, despising the shame, and hath sat down at the right hand of the throne of God." But although thus introduced in a merely incidental manner, our text has distinct doctrinal value, and is of the utmost importance as displaying the secret of that wondrous

[1] Rev. v. 12.

fortitude that distinguished Christ's suffering on the Cross, and revealing the cause of that triumphant cry, " It is finished,"[2] with which, in the very moment of apparent defeat, He hailed and announced to an astonished world a marvellous victory. We have seen what His obedience on the Cross was, have obtained some idea of its measure and its absolutely self-denying character ; but now a new light shines in upon the scene, and we behold His obedience not merely as submission to a terrible fate, but as the expression of the highest wisdom—a wisdom that threw not life away in recklessness, but gave in order to receive, expended in order to gain, endured in order to enjoy. And when we look at the matter in this new light, we are enabled more fully and clearly to apprehend the spirit in which our Lord entered upon and passed through the experiences that culminate in the Cross. There are two topics presented for our consideration in this passage, and these may be expressed thus :—

> 1st. The suffering of the Cross, and what was involved in it : " endured the Cross, despising the shame " ;
>
> 2nd. The animating issue that sustained the Saviour in this Cross-endurance : "the joy .. set before Him."

In the first place then I ask your attention to *the suffering of the Cross, and what was involved in it:*—" endured the Cross, despising the shame." There are three distinct elements in this suffering to which it is necessary we should have our thoughts turned in order that we may fully appreciate the whole. We must remember that our Saviour was human in

[2] John xix. 30.

every particular—human as well as divine—human in body, soul, and spirit, as much a man as man ever was, and as capable of human feelings and experiences—remorse for sin excepted—as man ever could be. It is necessary to say this at the outset, for there has ever been a tendency to present a view of the sufferings of Christ that disregards one or other of the parts of His nature. For example I saw the other day a notice of some very early representations of the crucifixion of our Lord—pictures carved and painted on precious material, and said to belong to not later than the 4th or 5th century. And what is remarkable about these representations is that there is no trace of suffering whatever on the face of the Christ as He hangs on the Cross, rather a sweet, placid aspect as if the body were not at all being racked with pain, and as if there were no physical experiences of suffering being passed through. Now it is well known that certain views relative to the person of Christ —views which denied the reality of His humanity—were prevailing at the time when these pictures were executed, and we simply see in them a reflex of these erroneous conceptions, and a denial of the cardinal truth which finds expression in this epistle from which we take our text; that "since then the children are sharers in flesh and blood, He also Himself in like manner partook of the same," that "not of angels doth He take hold, but He taketh hold of the seed of Abraham," that "it behoved Him in all things to be made like unto His brethren," and that as the Author of our salvation He was perfected through sufferings."[3] A much more just view of the nature of Christ have those, who like

[3] Heb. ii. 10, 14, 16, 17.

Raphael and Rubens and Tintoretto, and other of the greatest of the world's artists, have represented the crucified Saviour under aspects which, whilst they reveal the perfection of His calm submission, also set forth the deathly agony which He endured for our sakes. For this, without doubt, was one of the elements of His experience upon the Cross, and it is an element which finds prominence in each of the gospel accounts of the crucifixion.

The physical anguish of cross-bearing almost defies description. It exceeded the worst forms of torture known to and practised upon men. The punishment in later times was wont to be preceded by scourging which lacerated and tore the muscles of the back, and this custom was, as we know, observed in the case of our Lord. The suffering in Crucifixion arose in part from the constrained and fixed position of the body, and of the outstretched arms. Acute pain was caused by every twitch or motion of the back, lacerated by the scourge, and of the hands and feet, pierced by the nails. These latter were, moreover, driven through parts where many sensitive nerves and sinews come together, some of which were mutilated, others violently crushed down. Inflammation of the wounds in both hands and feet speedily set in, and supervened as well in other places, where the circulation was checked by the tension of the parts. Intolerable thirst, and ever increasing pain, resulted. The blood, which could no longer reach the extremities, rose to the head, swelled unnaturally the veins and arteries in it, and caused the most agonising tortures in the brain. As, besides, the heart could no longer move freely from the lungs, it grew more and more oppressed, and all the veins in the body were distended. Had the wounds bled freely, it would have been a great relief, but very little blood was lost. The weight of the body itself, resting on the wooden pin of the upright beam; the burning heat of the sun scorching the veins, and the hot wind, which dried up the moisture of the body, made each moment more terrible than that before. The numbness and stiffness of the more distant muscles brought on painful convulsions, and this numbness, slowly extending, at last reached the vital parts, when the sufferer was mercifully released by death.[4] Such is the description which has been given of the mere physical suffering which was wont to attend this awful mode of execution, and it is sufficiently appalling to make us shrink even from the contemplation of the details. But our recoil from these terrible features must not be such that we shall fail to realise that the Lord Jesus suffered them every one. And He suffered them in a frame more refined and pure, and so, more susceptible of pain, than was ever body borne by guilty man, for it was a frame untainted by sin, and so neither dulled nor rendered coarse by its preceding contact with evil. He was delicate as a woman and tender as a child, yet through all this He passed. And He passed through it, even refusing the proffered " wine mingled with myrrh "[5] that would have dulled the senses to the keenness of the agony. Even on its physical side Christ will endure all, endure it to the last pang, and the sorrowful end. The very fact that He would not take the opiate that was brought to His lips, is enough to show us that we must not neglect in our estimate of His sufferings the

[4] See Geikie, *The Life and Words of Christ*, Chap. lviii.
[5] Mark xv. 23.

bodily anguish through which He passed. There is meaning in this, and surely the poet has well expressed it:

> "Thou wilt feel all, that Thou mayst pity all;
> And rather wouldst Thou wrestle with strong pain,
>   Than overcloud Thy soul,
>   So clear in agony,
> Or lose one glimpse of Heaven before the time.
> O most entire and perfect sacrifice,
>   Renewed in every pulse
>   That on the tedious Cross
> Told the long hours of death, as, one by one,
> The life-strings of that tender heart gave way." [6]

But whilst we may not neglect the physical pain endured by our Lord in any consideration of His sufferings on the Cross, we must not imagine that this was the worst of His experiences. The apostle here singles out a special feature that calls for some attention. He records that "He despised the shame." Now in the former discourse we saw what a degrading death that on the cross was, and, by the contemporaries of our Lord was esteemed to be. Cicero declares that it "should never come near the thoughts, the eyes, or ears of a Roman citizen, far less his person." "It was the punishment inflicted by heathenism, which knew no compassion or reverence for man as man—on the worst criminals, on highway robbers, rebels and slaves, or on provincials who, in the eyes of Rome, were only slaves, if they fell into crime." [7] The special shame of the cross was that it stamped its victim in the sight of men as a notorious malefactor. And it is of this moral shame which we must think when we endeavour to realise what Christ endured, and what for the sake of us, He rose superior to. He took the opprobrium of the worst of sinners upon Himself. He permitted Himself

[6] Keble, *The Christian Year.* [7] Geikie, *Supra.*

to be treated as if He were the criminal of all criminals, the most abandoned and profligate wretch which the world had ever seen. There were thieves crucified on either side and "Jesus in the midst."[8] What a pre-eminence was this that was thrust upon Him! what an elevation in disgrace! what a crowning with the thorns of man's reproach. And He felt it all; for when He is represented as despising the shame, that does not mean that He did not experience or realise in all its bitterness the ignominy cast upon Him. Even we, who are guilty, would feel to be traduced and treated as the chief of criminals, how much more He who was "holy, guileless, undefiled."[9] We may rest assured that all the tortures of His body were as nothing to this torture which was passed through by His soul. The shadows grew dense about Him, when the mockery that assailed His ears, from priest and Pharisee, held Him up to derision as the blackest of sinners whom God had abandoned, and showed Him that, in place of pitying glances, those around His Cross in great numbers at least "did esteem Him, stricken, smitten of God and afflicted."[10]

But a deeper darkness gathers around the Sufferer on the Cross even than that occasioned to His spirit by the fact that by man He is treated as a transgressor. For there can be no doubt that the most profound experience of His agony was that which wrung from His lips the mysterious cry, "My God, My God, why hast Thou forsaken Me?"[11] And if this solemn cry is to be interpreted in the most simple, and yet, as it must be confessed, the most striking and significant way, it means no less than, that in the moment in which it was

[8] John xix. 18. [9] Heb. vii. 26. [10] Isa. liii. 4. [11] Mat. xxvii. 46.

uttered, Jesus had a sense of the turning from Him of the light of His Father's countenance. And what was this save an experience that He was being treated by God in a similar way to that in which He was being treated by man— viz., as one who was the chief of sinners? The shadow which in that awful experience veiled from Him the Father's face was no doubt the very same shadow which has, from all the human race, in their alienation, taken away the lustre of the divine countenance. No other cloud could come between God and any who stand related to Him; and so it seems very certain that in this supreme hour of suffering Christ was being "made to be sin on our behalf."[12] If so, how heart-rending must have been His experience! Terrible for Him indeed that He, the pure and spotless One, should by men be regarded as if He were the most wicked of all; but a thousandfold more terrible that He should have the feeling as if He were so regarded by His Heavenly Father! Into the depths of this it is utterly impossible that we can enter in thought; it exceeds the anguish which we would experience were our nearest and dearest to look upon us with abhorrence, and to treat us as if we had been guilty of the worst of crimes. No wonder that, as the blood and water that flowed from His pierced side evidenced, our Saviour died, not from the ordinary agonies of crucifixion, but from a broken heart.[13] He was surcharged with sorrow, and, by as far as the moral shame of being treated as a malefactor by the hands of men went beyond the physical pain of His Cross-bearing, by so far—if not even farther—went the

---

[12] 2 Cor. v. 21.
[13] Stroud, *Treatise on the Physical cause of the Death of Christ.*

anguish of His sense of separation from the Father's favour, even for a moment, beyond the grief of the ignominy which was heaped upon Him by His fellows. This ruptured the cords of His loving breast, and brought Him to the darkness of death. And yet it can be truly said that His endurance was finished ere He left the Cross; for even the broken heart had a strange final peace and calm, in which it commended the departing spirit to the divine hands:

> "Love masters Agony; the soul that seemed
> Forsaken, feels her present God again,
> And in her Father's arms
> Contented dies away." [14]

Such then, to its final throb, was the suffering of the Cross, and all this, and no less than this, was involved in it; thus He "endured the Cross despising the shame."

But we must turn now in the second place to consider *the animating issue that sustained the Saviour in this Cross-endurance:*—"the joy .. set before Him." In our Saviour's high-priestly prayer uttered on the very eve of His crucifixion we find a reference to this object, which is here, by the apostle, said to have had such an upholding and triumphing effect in the supreme crisis of our Lord's work. "I glorified Thee on the earth," says the divine Suppliant, "having accomplished the work which Thou hast given Me to do: and now, O Father, glorify Thou me with Thine own Self with the glory which I had with Thee before the world was." [15] And it was the assurance that this prayer of His would be answered, that He would regain all—nay far more than all the lustre that He had laid aside, when He "emptied Himself," or "made Himself of no reputation," [16] it was this assurance

[14] Keble, *Supra*.   [15] John xvii. 4, 5.   [16] Phil. ii. 7.

that bore Him up amidst the "sea of troubles" that assailed Him on the Cross, and enabled Him to breast the waves thereof and to conquer them, and thus to gain the victory through suffering. The principle which is here exemplified is not unfamiliar to us. We know how often men are willing to sacrifice present enjoyment of good, for future prospects of better; nay, how they will endure long years of toil, and privation, and hardship, for the sake of some object fitted to reward all their efforts. They can wait for their recompense, and even suffer in order that at last they may attain it. Now it was exactly thus with our Saviour on the Cross. The goal of glory—bright beyond all the dreams of earth, exalted above all that man or fallen angel could offer, was ever before His eyes. He could have had temporal power and honour had He wished—the Devil offered Him all these in the temptation [17] —He could have had the purple of earthly sovereignty, and the golden sceptre of world-wide rule, in place of the Cross of Calvary with its blood-drops and its thorn-crown; but there was a loftier position within His grasp than aught of earthly renown, and a wider dominion before His eyes than the most extensive worldly kingdom, and so He chose the Cross on Calvary for the sake of the crown in heaven, and renounced the pomp of time—electing rather its shame—for the sake of the glory which thereby would accrue to Him through all eternity. He endured with patience, "for the joy that was set before Him." This was the spirit in which He suffered, and the object which carried Him, a Conqueror, through it all.

But it may be asked, Does not this contemplation of

[17] Mat iv. 8, 9.

recompense on the part of our Lord bear a somewhat sordid aspect? In view of the glory that must be won by it, is not the self-renunciation of our Lord self-aggrandisement after all? If this was the sustaining element in His sufferings is not His Cross-endurance robbed of some of that aspect of disinterestedness which we are usually wont to associate with it? It is not difficult to give an answer to these questions. Indeed we find the answer already in that prayer of our Lord to which we have already referred, for does He not say in it, "Father, I will that they also whom Thou hast given Me, be with Me where I am: that they may behold My glory."[18] This beholding of the glory of Christ carries with it the eternal felicity and salvation of those who are so privileged. Indeed they are sharers with Him in the lustre of it; it is reflected in the exaltation and the happiness of their condition. Still more, it really arises from their redemption—it is the glory of the victorious Saviour, a glory which could not be, unless the trophies of His loving power were there to shed forth its light. The "joy set before" the divine Sufferer was no other than the joy of beholding the effect of these sufferings in the manifold triumphs of His redeeming grace over the hearts and lives of men. His joy was to "see the travail of His soul and be satisfied,"[19] it was to ascend to heaven leading captivity captive and receiving gifts *of* men,[20] it was to bring many sons unto glory,[21] in a word, the joy set before Him was to accomplish all His gracious purposes, and the gracious purposes of His Father, relative to the human race—to accomplish these, by bringing back to the heavenly

[18] John xvii. 24.   [19] Isa. liii. 11.
[20] Ps. lxviii. 18; See Carl Bernhard Moll's *Commentary on the Psalms.*   [21] Heb. ii. 10.

home the lost children of men, making them once more children of His heavenly Father, and exalting them to co-heirship with Himself of all the blessings that belong to this sacred condition. And when we have this view of the object which our Lord had before His eyes in His Cross-endurance, and by which he was sustained and animated therein, at once it is manifest to us, that there is nothing sordid or selfish in His having respect to such a recompense, but on the contrary the most absolute disinterestedness, the most pure and noble benevolence. And we find especially that the root of His patience is not self-aggrandisement, but love —love for those whom He came to seek and to save. His joy in them and their joy in Him are what sustain His heart amidst unparalleled suffering ; for it is destined to grow out of such suffering—its sure blossom and fruit. It no longer amazes us that Christ should endure the Cross for the sake of the throne when we learn that thereon He is to rule over countless hosts of the redeemed with the sceptre of love. He may well wear the crown of thorns who is thereby to be eternally crowned in His people's hearts.

Dense is the darkness that gathers around the Cross of Christ ; it is the darkest spot in the world's history : and yet it is the most hopeful scene that ever transpired on this earth of ours. If it brings us to the depths, it leads us away to the heights—if there be no suffering, no sorrow, no degradation more profound than that which it exhibits, there is no felicity, no joy, no glory more exalted than that to which at last it guides. And this felicity, joy, glory, form the destined portion not only of Him who suffers there, but of all who suffer in and with Him. Those who are constrained to the cross will assuredly be led to the crown. It is yours and mine to determine whether we shall restrict or enhance the lustre and happiness of Him who dies there. Every one, brought to His Cross in contrition, is an augmenter of His joy, every trophy of His redeeming grace adds to the brightness of His crown. Contemplate all He endured on your behalf, and then declare whether by unbelief you will defraud Him of the fulness of His reward. These sufferings have been revealed in all their extent and depth in order that they may captivate your hearts, and lead you to ask, What return can I make for such a sacrifice on my behalf? As you well know there is only one return which He desires, and that is, that through your love meeting this expression of His, you surrender yourselves to Him for the furtherance of His glory and joy, and thereby for the furtherance of your own. Would you have part in that glad festal scene in which the completed triumphs of the kingdom shall be celebrated? then let the Cross of Christ draw you on to it. Whoever in faith beholds the thorn-crowned Head bowed in death, shall have the beatific vision of the Son of Man exalted above the clouds of heaven and seated on the throne of His glory. God grant that we all may with joy, and not with terror, be spectators of this sight; that we may be of the number who hail the Lord Jesus when He appears in all the fulness of His lustre, and who sing before Him the pæan of welcome and victory:

> " Ah come, Thou blessèd One,
> God's own belovèd Son;
> Hallelujah!
> We follow till the halls we see,
> Where Thou hast bid us sup with Thee.

THE JOY SET BEFORE HIM.

Now let all the heavens adore Thee,
And men and angels sing before Thee
    With harp and cymbal's clearest tone ;
Of one pearl each shining portal,
Where we are with the choir immortal
    Of angels round Thy dazzling throne ;
    Nor eye hath seen, nor ear
    Hath yet attained to hear,
      What there is ours ;
But we rejoice and sing to Thee
Our hymn of joy eternally." [22]

[22] Philip Nicolai, translated by Catherine Winkworth.

III.
PEACE THROUGH THE BLOOD.

My Lord, my Love, was crucified ;
   He all the pains did bear ;
But in the sweetness of His rest
   He makes His servants share.
How sweetly rest Thy saints above
   Which in Thy bosom lie !
The Church below doth rest in hope
   Of that felicity.

   .   .   .   .   .

I bless Thy wise and wondrous love,
   Which binds us to be free ;
Which makes us leave our earthly snares,
   That we may come to Thee !
I come, I wait, I hear, I pray !
   Thy footsteps, Lord, I trace !
I sing to think this is the way
   Unto my Saviour's face !—J. MASON.

THE CROSS OF CHRIST.

III.—PEACE THROUGH THE BLOOD.

Colossians I. 20—"Having made peace through the blood of His Cross."

In the two discourses which have preceded I have dealt with the spirit in which our Lord suffered upon the Cross—the spirit of obedience, "became obedient unto death, even the death of the Cross," and the spirit of patient anticipation, "Who for the joy that was set before Him, endured the Cross, despising the shame." To-day we are brought to a different phase of this great theme, and enter upon consideration of the purpose of Christ's sufferings as that is presented in the New Testament passages that make mention of His Cross. As I have already indicated there are three such passages—*first*, that which is this afternoon before us; *second*, the words in the Epistle to the Ephesians, "Reconcile both unto God in one body by the Cross;"[1] and *lastly*, the statement made in the 2nd chapter of the Epistle which contains our text, which in respect of the accusation or indictment by the law against us, declares that our Saviour "took it out of the way, nailing it to His Cross."[2] These three important and significant apostolic expressions of verity have certain close and essential relations to each

[1] Eph. ii. 16.   [2] Col. ii. 14.

other, so that, superficially viewed, they might almost be regarded as but slightly varied representations of one and the same truth. They all more or less directly deal with the removal of barriers that had existed between God and man, and place the Cross of Christ before us as the efficient means of securing this result. But when we examine these passages with some degree of care, and get to apprehend them in connection with their textual surroundings, we find that they are not mere repetitions of the same thought, but that they have each a distinct message relative to the Cross of Christ to convey to us, and that the measure of their diversity—not their *disharmony*, be it remarked,—is greater than the measure of their identity. Each of them emphasises some special phase of gospel truth that is not so prominently set forth by either of the others, and therefore despite the intimate relation between them they may with advantage be treated separately ; and, in this way, we shall most clearly bring before our minds as well the specific spiritual facts which they individually establish, and the comprehensive and far-reaching views of the gospel which they unitedly present.

It might seem more in accordance with the proper order of things to begin our consideration of the purpose of Christ's sufferings by an examination of that passage that records how He has taken the accusation which was against us out of the way, nailing it to His Cross, for undoubtedly this lies at the root of the truths set forth in the other two. But it is legitimate, as well as more usual, to go back from results to causes rather than forward from causes to results, and in the present instance we have a special authority, or, shall we say example ? for adopting a course that brings us at once into contact with the final and most comprehensive purpose of the Cross of Christ. For this final and comprehensive purpose was the great and glorious theme of the very first gospel song that sounded forth after the advent of the Redeemer. The herald angel and the multitude of the heavenly host, who praised God above the plains of Bethlehem, sang of peace on earth, good will towards men. [3] This, we may say, was the first note of the evangel, its earliest message brought to men, the primary chord struck from heavenly harps and destined to resound through all time and into eternity; the first and yet also the last, the dominant theme, which is to be maintained through all the varied harmonies of gospel music until the very end, and which shall be taken up and re-echoed in the new heaven and the new earth, when peace shall be finally and for ever established and all discords shall have died away. It is therefore befitting that we should begin our study of the purpose of our Saviour's sufferings with these words which tell us of His "having made peace through the blood of His Cross."

Now, in respect of the truth set forth in our text, I have to observe at the outset that PEACE-MAKING PRESUPPOSES A PRE-CEDING DISPEACE. There is no need to bring about harmony if there has not been discord—no need to secure calm and quiet and rest if there has not been turmoil and storm and strain. It is therefore necessary for the understanding of our text that we should seek at the outset to apprehend the condition which it implicitly assumes to have existed prior to the setting up of the Cross of Christ—not prior it may be in time but prior in the order of spiritual conception—and which the setting up

[3] Luke ii. 14.

of that Cross remedied, or the termination of which was thereby made possible. The several points therefore that call for consideration are :—

> 1st. What elements of dispeace were there, in order to the removal of which, Christ shed His blood on Calvary?
>
> 2nd. What contrasting condition did that shedding of blood ensure to man?
>
> 3rd. How is it that such a contrasting condition—viz., a condition of peace as against that of dispeace—is secured "through the blood of His Cross"?

These are the three questions that come before us to-day, and to the first of which we must now specially direct attention.

First then, *What elements of dispeace were there, in order to the removal of which Christ shed His blood on Calvary?* In the verse that succeeds that which contains our text we have the chief cause of man's dispeace—the root of all the unrest of his heart and life—set forth in suggestive language. The apostle says of those to whom he was writing, and his words have application to all mankind, "You that were sometime alienated, and enemies in your mind by wicked works."[4] He does not merely call them aliens, as if they had been always that, but alienated, to mark an historical fact. A foreigner is an alien, he has never been anything else, he has been born such, but a fellow-citizen may become alienated, that is, through disloyalty and rebellion he may become estranged in spirit, in aim, and in his whole life, from his native land. A stranger is an alien to the circle of our

[4] Col. i. 21.

friendship, he has never been in it, and that he is out of it is no reflection upon him at all; but a friend may become alienated, that is, having been within the circle of friendship, he may through unfriendliness and betrayal have sundered himself from it and cast himself out of it. And these illustrations will show what the apostle means when he writes of man as alienated from God. He refers, as I have said, to an historical fact. The friend of God has become the enemy, the mind formerly in harmony with the mind of God has become estranged, the life at one time in concord with His life has become absolutely incompatible therewith through its evil works. And this historical fact, which is so suggestively placed before us by the apostle in the context, is the cause of man's dispeace, or to put it more generally the cause of all the dispeace between God and man, and the cause as well of all unrest and disquiet that flow therefrom.

Dispeace between God and man is undoubtedly the chief evil. For when we consider the relative positions of those who are thus out of accord with each other we cannot but admit that, so far at least as man is concerned, this variance is wholly disastrous and calamitous. It is a quarrel that can be fraught with nothing but harm to the human race, for it has brought into antagonism forces that are as widely disproportionate to each other as we can well imagine opposing elements to be. The puny arm of the creature raised in rebellion against the omnipotent hand of the Creator; the worm of the dust defying and contending with Him whose word alone could crush it, as we with the heel can destroy a crawling reptile; the potsherd of the earth striving with his Maker. What can be the possible issue of such dispeace save utter ruin and misery to our weak humanity?

But even apart from this, its final issue, if it go on unchecked, the passing experience of man whilst this dispeace continues, can be nothing but evil. It is in the light of the divine countenance that his happiness can alone be found. And, just as when the face of a friend is beclouded, there follow, to such as have enjoyed its former favour, misery and disquiet, so there has entered into human experience, through this rupture with God, the deepest woe and the worst ills. It is not indeed the general wont of man to trace up to this cause the evils which he has more or less fully to endure. Unbelief admits those evils, but either makes them a mere necessity of our earthly condition—which be it remarked is no explanation at all; or sets them down to man's inhumanity to man—which is but a partial account of their origin, and, in so far as it is an account at all, is a tracing of them up to merely secondary sources, instead of referring them to their great primal root; that root being no other than the breaking of amity between man and God.

As a matter of fact, this cardinal dispeace, which through sin has become the heritage of the human race, is the bitter fountainhead of all human ills. For, from the primary dispeace, there flow other phases of disharmony which are laden with untold evils. Man is not only out of accord with God, he is also thereby made out of accord with all who are morally and spiritually united to God. There is dispeace between man and the angels, that is, between man and those bright intelligences who constantly obey the divine behests and delight to do the divine will. And how much evil this entails we cannot compute. To lose the services of these ministering spirits, to have no help in any extremity from the angels of God, and to have as well the continual harassment of the wrong-doing and the harm-bringing of those angels who kept not their first estate, is not this to incur an immeasurable degree of evil? We have become so materialistic and unspiritual in our conceptions that this element of damage, which through the rupture of our communion with God we have sustained, is apt to be lost sight of. We forget that through our rebellion we have not only paralysed the powers of the heavenly host that might for ever have been exerted in our favour, but have arrayed against us the innumerable company of angels who people the universe and are messengers of the divine will, whilst we have by no means gained, in any way that tells for good, the aid of those high fallen intelligences through whose temptations we at first lapsed into sin.

But yet again I remark, that dispeace with God has carried with it into human history the dispeace of man with man. So long as our minds were in harmony with the divine mind they must have been of necessity in harmony with each other, but the moment disunion here occurred, the floodgates of mutual enmity and discord were opened wide. Righteousness is oneness, sin is legion. Those who are righteous cannot but be in accord; those who are sinful have thousand-fold possibilities of strife. Hence all the ill which man has done to man through enmity is traceable up to this original source of dispeace with God. All the miseries, the pains, the anguish, the sufferings of every kind, that have come to man through wars, through treacheries, through feuds, through selfishness, through ruptured friendships, through betrayed trusts, through enmities; all the bitterness, and heartburning, and wrong; in short all the ills in every shape and form which man has inflicted on his fellow-man, come without exception from this primal root. It has indeed been fertile in fruits of the most poisonous and joy-destroying nature: out of it there have grown strifes, envies, jealousies, malice, anger, deceit, murder, spoliation, yea every form of social evil that has cursed the human race. It has been the fountainhead of waters, as bitter as those of Marah, that have flowed in full flood, from the shut gate of Eden, down through all the centuries of man's history to the present day.

But once more dispeace with God has carried with it dispeace with nature. "Cursed is the ground for thy sake ... thorns also and thistles shall it bring forth to thee."[5] Whatever of the literal we may understand by this, there is much more in the figurative application of which it is susceptible. When man fell out of accord with God he fell out of accord with his surroundings. These arrayed themselves against him. The lower creatures, over whom, as the crown of creation, he had been set, became his enemies; the ground, which he had tilled with ease in paradise, he had now to labour upon in the sweat of his face and the sorrow of his heart. It would indeed seem as if to this primal root of dispeace with God we must trace up all the ravages of wild beasts and untamed nature, all the grime and toil and torture of ill-requited work, all the evils incident to oppression for the sake of gain, all the hardship and care and weariness of human life that struggles to maintain itself amidst adverse surroundings; the furrowed brow, the whitened hair, the

[5] Gen. iii. 17, 18.

tottering limbs, the bowed back, the dull eyes, the feeble step, and, last of all, the premature grave, that closes man's little day of labour, and gives only a shadowed rest that brings no recompense for manifold toils.

But lastly—for we must bring this part of our subject to a close—dispeace with God has carried with it dispeace with ourselves. Man is not in harmony with his own heart. There are gnawing troubles within him which he can refer to none of the secondary forms of unrest of which I have spoken. The soul that is out of harmony with the divine is all jangled and out of tune. Its greatest happiness is to forget itself, and this is the secret of its continual panting and striving after objects that will make it oblivious, and is the cause of its ceaseless question and cry, "Who will shew us any good?"[6] The fact is, the worm in man's bosom dieth not, and the fire is not quenched. His rupture with God has brought about a strife in his own nature which he cannot by any effort of his own compose. "There is no peace, saith my God, to the wicked."[7]

I have now endeavoured to answer the first question that is brought before us by our text, viz.—What elements of dispeace exist, for the removal of which, Christ shed His blood on Calvary? And I have now to ask your attention in the second place to *the contrasting condition which through His Cross-bearing Christ has made possible for man.* It will not be necessary to enter into detail as I have done in the preceding considerations, for, in the first place, we have just to present to our minds a picture the reverse of all that has been said, in order to realise the boon which Christ has secured for us, and then,

[6] Ps. iv. 6.   [7] Isa. lvii. 21.

further, we shall have occasion in a subsequent discourse to bring out certain features of this contrasting condition which may be here merely alluded to. The main purpose I have in view at this stage is to indicate the necessity that existed for peace-making, and thereby to bring out with the requisite fulness the glorious purpose which our Lord had before Him, and which he accomplished, through the shedding of His blood on the Cross at Calvary. I think it will be admitted that the state of man was sufficiently deplorable to call for the utmost efforts being put forth to secure for him a treaty of peace. To be absolutely out of harmony with God, with the universe, with self, was to be in the worst condition of which we can conceive. Most worthy then was the aim of the Son of God. It was to remove whatever elements of enmity existed in the relation of man to God; it was to bring man into accord with all those who were in harmony with the divine will; it was to institute a brotherhood of the human race, that all the evils incident to the discords which prevail between man and man might disappear; it was to hasten on the time when even nature should be brought into sweet unison with man's interests, and in the new heaven and the new earth "the whole creation" that "groaneth and travaileth in pain together until now" should be "delivered from the bondage of corruption into the liberty of the glory of the children of God;"[8] and finally it was to still the troubles of man's own heart and life and to bring to him the peace that "passeth all understanding," which the world cannot give and the world cannot take away.[9] And all these things, Christ has through the blood of His Cross

---

[8] Rom. viii. 21, 22.   [9] Phil. iv. 7.

rendered possible of accomplishment. For a reason yet to be given, man need no longer stand alienated from his Maker. The treaty of peace, signed and sealed with the blood that dropped on Calvary, secures the entrance of the vilest sinner into the presence of the heavenly Father, and guarantees his pardon and acceptance. That same treaty has enlisted the whole angelic host in man's service. Angels and archangels are no longer arrayed against us :—" Are they not all ministering spirits, sent forth to minister for them who shall be heirs of salvation?"[10] The same treaty has also brought about such a community of character and aim between man and man, in so far as they come under its influence, that all contentions and strifes may have an end, and the universal reign of amity and love may well begin. And then further, does not this treaty of peace restore man to paradise? It removes not indeed the literal curse from the ground here, but it enables us to toil on, in hope, in view of the hereafter—that hereafter which embraces a new Eden to every believer as soon as he or she has crossed the swellings of the Jordan, and which bears with it the promise of a higher and better condition than that of paradise, by giving an abundant entrance into heaven, on the resurrection morn. And then finally, this treaty of peace is fitted to take away out of our human lives every element that can shadow them, the worm that gnaws and the fire that scorches, the remorse that devours and the reproach that burns, the lusts that war in the soul, and the body of death that enchains the spirit. It is no mere outward peace that it brings, but a gracious quiet that reigns to the depths of the human heart, and secures

[10] Heb. i. 14.

there the most perfect content. To make use of the old and priceless Scriptural terms it secures sanctification as well as justification. Such is the contrasting condition into which, through the blood of His Cross, Christ has made it possible for man to be brought. I say, *made it possible*, for, after all, the issue rests with each individual for himself rather than with Christ. The Saviour has made the treaty of peace; it is for you to say if you accept that treaty. He has made it for all, but there may be rebels still. The amnesty may be refused, the terms of the compact repudiated, the covenant itself cast down and trampled under foot. Alas! that in any case it should be so, but it is only too certain that for some at least the blood of Christ has been shed in vain.

I must now, however, pass on, in the last place, to the consideration of the final point which our text brings before us, *How it is that this contrasting condition—the condition of peace as against that of dispeace—is brought about or secured "through the blood of His Cross."* Peace through blood—that is the strange problem before us—nay, peace through the blood of the Cross: a problem stranger still. Has not blood been the cause of aught but peace amongst the human race? Has not vengeance again and again risen to demand the price of blood, and exacted that price to the uttermost drop? And would we not imagine that blood shed in the way in which the blood of Christ was shed—blood shed on the Cross—blood shed in so degrading and shameful a way—and the blood of One so innocent and pure and yet thus shed, would everlastingly call for revenge? Of the first drop of human blood shed upon the earth God said to the murderer, "The voice of thy brother's blood crieth unto me from the ground;"[11] would it have been at all surprising if the message to those who crucified Christ—and that is the message to man as man—had been, This blood cries from Golgotha to heaven for vengeance against the human race? But truly the apostle has well said of the blood of Christ that it "speaketh better things than that of Abel."[12] It cries not for vengeance but for mercy, it invokes not judgment but grace, it calls not for condemnation but pardon. As the very first drops of it fall to the earth on Calvary, the divine Sufferer says, " Father, forgive them ; for they know not what they do."[13] Truly this blood of the Cross is mysterious in its contrast to all the blood that has ever been shed in other circumstances by man, and we must seek to unravel the problem it presents.

What is at the root of all the dispeace which the human race suffers and has suffered, and which is said to be made capable of removal by the blood of the Cross? It is *sin.* This is the short but all-sufficient explanation of the discord between man and God, and of all evils and miseries thence proceeding. But in respect of sin there is a great moral and spiritual law existing in the universe, applicable to this earth of ours, illustrated through the sacrifices of the more ancient economy, and expressed directly in the sacred word, as well as indirectly assumed by our Lord and His apostles, and that law is " Without shedding of blood is no remission."[14] And this means that without blood there is no removal of the root and cause of dispeace between God and man, and no possibility of reunion and harmony between the human and

[11] Gen. iv. 10. [12] Heb. xii. 24. [13] Luke xxiii. 34.
[14] Heb. ix. 22, compare Mat. xxvi. 28.

the divine. This is the key to the blood of the Cross as the great peace-making element. It is not the suffering of any and every one that can secure the end in view. The Lamb of God alone bears away the sin of the world.[15] In Christ, God has secured Himself a Victim for the sacrifice. "Christ our passover is sacrificed for us."[16] It is because He suffers as a sacrifice and expiation, and for that reason alone, that His blood calls down upon our humanity mercy and not judgment. It is this that lies at the basis of our text and makes it an everlasting verity, so that, to the vision of faith, Christ may appear to-day, and may appear through all time, to those who have need of Him, as "making peace through the blood of His Cross."

The Cross of Christ is thus the guarantee of the highest blessing which man can wish or God bestow. We behold for what high and holy end it was erected at Calvary. As out of the dark ground the fairest lily may grow, so out of this sad and shadowed scene there spring up for man the richest blossom and fruit of spiritual life. Christ's suffering is your salvation, Christ's troubles are your peace.

> "Peace, perfect peace, in this dark world of sin?
> The blood of Jesus whispers peace within."[17]

If you desire this blessed experience, it is yours if you but, in faith, make a journey to the place called Golgotha. Thereafter, the Cross of Christ, though once the scene of such awful agony, will be for ever to you the symbol of eternal calm. The precious inheritance which Christ has left to his disciples will become your portion: "Peace I leave with you, my peace I give unto you."[18] And as the depths of the

---

[15] John i. 29.
[16] 1 Cor. v. 7.   [17] Bishop Bickersteth.   [18] John xiv. 27.

ocean are still unruffled though the surface be lashed into fury by the storm, so there shall be depths in your life which no tempest of time can disquiet, and which eternity itself shall but confirm. This is the peace of the Cross—

> "Not as the world hath given,
> In momentary rays that fitful gleamed,
> But calm, deep, sure,—the peace of spirits shriven,
> Of hearts surrendered, and of souls redeemed.
> Grant us Thy peace, that, like a deepening river,
> Swells ever onward to a sea of praise:
> O Thou, of peace the only Lord and Giver,
> Grant us Thy peace, our Saviour, all our days." [19]

[19] Eliza Scudder.

IV.
RECONCILIATION BY THE CROSS.

Christ's Cross is the christ-cross of all our happiness; it delivers us from all blindness of error, and enriches our darkness with light; it restoreth the troubled soul to rest; it bringeth strangers to God's acquaintance; it maketh remote foreigners near neighbours; it cutteth off discord; concludeth a league of everlasting peace, and is the bounteous author of all good.

—AUGUSTINE.

THE CROSS OF CHRIST.

IV.—*RECONCILIATION BY THE CROSS.*

Ephesians II. 16—"That He might reconcile both unto God in one body by the Cross, having slain the enmity thereby."

"Peace on earth," peace secured through the blood of the Cross of Christ—that was the theme of our meditation last Sabbath afternoon. And to-day we are brought to the consideration of a passage that deals with what is practically the same subject, but with a different aspect of it, and in a wholly different connection. The topic itself is one that may be regarded as inexhaustible, and, even were our standpoint on this occasion the same as that which we occupied in last discourse, we would find no lack of variety in the questions and conceptions that might be brought before us. For we have only been able to touch upon those features that belong to the peace that flows like the broad volume of a river from the Cross of Christ, not by any means to enquire into and dwell upon them with that fulness which their importance merits. There are far-reaching effects of the blood of the Cross in this region which we have not even had opportunity to refer to—effects upon the universe, upon the world, upon human society, and upon individual life; the universal reign of peace which Christ shall at last, through his completed work, establish ere He gives up the kingdom into the hands of His Father; the gradually extending influence of peace in the progress of history over the earth; the gracious triumphs of peace in the social relationships of man with man; the various developments of peace that come to us through faith in and following of Christ—mental peace, moral peace, spiritual peace, peace of the intellect, peace of the emotions, peace of the will; peace in the heart, peace in the brain, peace in the soul—these, and other kindred aspects of truth, might well have occupied our attention even in dealing with the general theme which our last text brought before us, for they are one and all phases of that comprehensive effect to which the apostle refers when he writes of Christ as "having made peace through the blood of His Cross." [1]

But it would require a volume and not a short discourse to overtake fully the topics which arise in connection with the series of passages we are considering, and, tempting as are the lines of spiritual truth that stretch out before us, we must content ourselves with mere glimpses of these outlying verities, whilst we emphasise the more prominent points that are directly placed before us by the particular texts which fall to be examined in the plan we are pursuing.

In order to place ourselves at the point of view which the apostle is occupying in the words to-day before us, we must give heed to the general argument of which they form part. He is writing to a Gentile church, and evidently desires to reassure the members thereof that they are under no disadvantage as compared with those who were formerly the chosen people of God. They had been at one time far off, not only separate from Christ, but alienated from the commonwealth

[1] Col. i. 20.

of Israel, strangers from the covenants of promise, having no hope, and without God in the world.[2] But all this had been changed, and changed through the work of the Saviour upon the Cross. For says the apostle "Now in Christ Jesus, ye that once were far off are made nigh in the blood of Christ." "For," he adds, "He is our Peace, Who hath made both one, and brake down the middle wall of partition, having abolished in His flesh the enmity, even the law of commandments contained in ordinances; that He might create in Himself of the twain one new man, so making peace; and might reconcile them both in one body unto God through the Cross, having slain the enmity thereby."[3] Our text, as you will observe, appears as a kind of culmination in this argument. Christ has through His Cross done something that He might pave the way for doing something else—through His Cross he has rendered possible the union of the divided, that by His Cross he might reconcile both to God—through His Cross He has broken down the hedge of separation between Jew and Gentile, that, having brought them together and made them coalesce in one body, He might bring them into harmony with His heavenly Father. This is the complex truth, partly expressed, partly presupposed in our text, which we must endeavour to apprehend if we would realise its teaching. And it will be best that we should examine this truth in its most general form, merely taking the specific example before us as an indication or illustration of certain issues of the Cross of Christ that are of much wider incidence and import. And this we shall, I think, accomplish if we direct our

[2] Eph. ii. 11, 12. [3] *Ibid* vv. 13-16.

attention to the following points, all of which are involved in our text, viz. :—

 1st. The unifying effect of the Cross of Christ : " both in one body ";

 2nd. Christ on the Cross the Representative of the entire human race : " that He might reconcile them both in one body to God "; and

 3rd. The Cross as the medium of the reconciliation of man to God : " reconcile them ... through the Cross."

The primary point then to which our attention is to be turned, is *the unifying effect of the Cross of Christ :* " both in one body." In one of the preceding verses you will notice that Christ is said to have broken down the middle wall of partition.[4] It is supposed that the apostle in this figure has in view the separation that had existed in the temple between the court of the Israelites and that of the Gentiles. That dividing wall was significant of a wide and almost impassable gulf that existed between these two sections of the human race. The one seemed, in respect of privilege and of relation to God, to be immeasurably far off as compared with the other. And the ostensible ground of this difference lay in the possession by Israel of a cluster of sacred ordinances that conferred on that people what one might call a priestly status. They were, at least through their appointed representatives, brought into a close and advantageous relation to God. On the other hand, those who did not belong to this nation had no such direct access; their approach to the divine was only through the privileged people—they might

[4] *Ibid* ver. 14.

become proselytes, proselytes of the gate or proselytes of righteousness, but even at the best, only proselytes, and not of so high religious standing as the genuine sons of Abraham. And from this there sprang an antagonism, a cleavage deep and wide, between Jew and Gentile, an enmity that prevented, and appeared for ever to render impossible, coalescence of these two elements.

It is evident however, that if the ground of this divergence should ever be removed, then the divergence itself would of necessity disappear. Now the truth presupposed in our text is that Christ has removed the entire basis of this old distinction. The Jewish ordinances were but temporal pictures or signs; they were never designed to be permanent realities, and, at the most, were only parables of great spiritual facts. It matters not though this was not realised by those who possessed them, and that the want of this realisation was the cause of a wider separation between Jew and Gentile than need have existed. If the meaning of the Mosaic economy had been preserved and fully apprehended by the nation, it would have been recognised that Israel had possession of the shadow of a substance that equally belonged to Jew and Gentile, and that God had blessed His people, and caused His face to shine upon them, that His way might be known upon the earth, His saving health among all nations. [5] But this was not realised in the ultimate history of Israel, and when our Saviour came, there was existing an exclusiveness, a pharisaic separatism, and a proud contempt for all outside of the pale of the chosen people, which, as Christ was not slow to indicate, was wholly out of accord with the spirit of a true faith.

[5] Ps. lxvii. 1, 2.

It was part of His great work to remove for ever the ground on which there might be even excuse for the growing up of such spiritual aloofness, and for the consequent division of humanity into two widely sundered classes. Through His Cross He brought the Gentile as nigh to God as the Jew; or, to speak more accurately, rendered it possible for the one to find as easy access as the other; placed them upon the same level or standing, so that the one should have no advantage over the other—the one no reason to plume himself upon special privilege, and the other no reason to lament disability or remoteness. And this He did, as the context tells us, by "abolishing in His flesh the enmity," that is "the law of commandments contained in ordinances." [6] The only meaning of which this remarkable statement seems to me susceptible is, that He in His Own body fulfilled to the very last degree, or perfectly, the spirit of these ordinances. They were symbols of sacrifice, offerings which, in a figure, represented the great oblation for sin; and, when the great oblation was itself made, the symbols or figures of necessity ceased to be of value and passed away. When He, the great Sacrifice for sin, had offered Himself up, there was no need of the continuation and repetition of the mere shadows which had existed as pictorial predictions of His saving work. As the author of the Epistle to the Hebrews has put it, "By one offering He hath perfected for ever them that are sanctified," so that there is fulfilment to them of the promise, "their sins and their iniquities will I remember no more." "Now," adds the inspired writer, "where remission of these is, there is no more offering for sin." [7] Thus the ground of distinction

[6] Eph. ii. 15. [7] Heb. x. 14, 17, 18.

between Jew and Gentile completely disappears, the partition wall is broken down, in the gospel church they mingle together, "one body" of which the Head is Christ. This unifying issue is one of the cardinal purposes which Christ had in view when He suffered the death of the Cross, and it was surely significant of it, that the hands both of Jews and Gentiles were imbrued in His blood, that, not the one to the exclusion of the other, but unitedly, though, no doubt, unconsciously, they placed this great Sacrifice on the world's high altar.

The only features about this unification through the Cross of Christ to which it is necessary for me at this stage to call attention are these two :—*First*, it was secured by the raising to a priestly status of those who had hitherto been, so to speak, in the outer court of the temple ; and, *second*, it was confirmed by the abasement of those who had arrogated to themselves a position of special sanctity to which they had no claim. After the Cross-endurance of our Lord, the Gentile might come even into the holiest of all, and, by faith, sprinkle with the blood of the perfect Sacrifice the mercy seat between the cherubim. Thus far was he admitted within a sphere from which he had been formerly excluded. But the great truth, and that for the sake of which it is worth emphasising this point in our text, is that every sinner, however far off he may be, may come through Christ as nigh as this. There is now no barrier between the transgressor—no matter how great the distance that lies between him and his God— there is now no barrier between him and the mercy seat. He may come from the outermost point of alienation, and find that there is no partition wall that excludes him from a position alongside of the most eminent and saintly of those who, through Christ, have been acceptable to God. He does not even require to perform, first, some work of purification for his admission to this sacred sphere, but rather must come just as he is, in all his sinfulness, however notorious, in all the guilt of his iniquity, however great. And if he so come, and come in contrition and faith, he shall find how absolutely the Cross of Christ has removed every obstacle out of his way, and shall find, as well, that he is as welcome as those who may not have gone so far astray, and that his return is hailed with acclamations that rise from earth to heaven, and sound around the throne of the Eternal; for is not this the testmony of the Master, the testimony of Him, Who is Himself the great acceptable and all-sufficing Sacrifice, "I say unto you, there is joy in the presence of the angels of God over one sinner that repenteth?"[8]

The other feature that calls for attention, in relation to the unification that is effected through the Cross of Christ, is the abasement of those who have arrogated to themselves a position of special sanctity to which they had no claim. If the death of Christ on the Cross elevates the sinful Gentile, it brings down the pharisaic Jew. For if it removes one barrier it seems, in a very striking way, to set up another, or rather, to accentuate that which to the self-righteous will appear as a forbidding obstacle. For it demands repentance, and it insists that all who come to the mercy seat with the blood of the new covenant, that is, with the blood of Christ, shall stand there on the same level. It knows no distinction of man and man in respect of approach into the presence of

[8] Luke xv. 10.

God. It does not admit that these may come with credentials of personal holiness, and be received of God, whilst those others must take their stand as delinquents and depend upon His mercy. The death of Christ declares that there is no difference. The one prayer which it puts in the mouths of all who would sincerely enter into the divine presence is " God, be merciful to me a sinner." [9] The most exalted Jew must here stand shoulder to shoulder with the most degraded Gentile. There is nothing more out of accord with the spirit of Christianity than aught that savours of sanctimoniousness; there is nothing which will more effectually exclude man from the holy of holies, and so from the sphere of the mercy seat, than the idea that he is himself holy. All that pride that *denies the one body*, that is, that denies the essential unity, through need of a like salvation, of those who are Christians, casts out its possessor from the pale of the faith by being itself cast out from the experience of the cleansing efficacy of the blood of Christ. What cleansing can they desire who have no consciousness of sin? There is no message for them from the Cross of Christ; there is no gospel to proclaim in their ears: Jesus Himself said, " I am not come to call the righteous but sinners to repentance." [10] There must be no denial then of this primary union of the human race, achieved through the Cross of Christ, on the part of any one who sincerely desires to have the benefits and blessings of that Cross. There must be recognition and acceptance of the fact that, to use the apostle's language, " the Scripture hath concluded all under sin." [11] Thus alone can there be acceptance for salvation, thus alone are we bound up in that

[9] Luke xviii. 13. [10] Luke v. 32. [11] Gal. iii. 22.

renovation of which the context speaks in these words which describe the purpose in its ultimate aim of Christ's Cross-bearing, "that He might create in Himself of the twain one new man, so making peace,"[12] and thus alone do we become partakers in all the privileges set forth and implied in the closing verses of the chapter which contains our text, and which declare the sacred and sure position of those who are in Christ Jesus. If we are united at the mercy seat by our common sinfulness, we shall be united afterwards by a common salvation, then by a common sanctification, and at last by a common glory. The one body, Christ will redeem, will purify, will exalt, but precisely in the same way as He with His Own personal body passed through these vicissitudes, in so far as they can be applied to him: first, humiliation and suffering, yea, even death; then, the upward progress from the grave to the throne; and finally, the everlasting lustre of the perfected condition. One body in Christ Jesus, that is the main theme of our text—made one through His Cross—the enmity between the different members of this one body slain through the slaying of Christ on the Cross—and this one body in its unity reconciled unto God by the Cross. Therefore, of all who are clasped together in this unity, we may well sing:—

> "To them the Cross, with all its shame,
>   With all its grace, is given;
> Their name, an everlasting name,
>   Their joy, the joy of heaven.
> They suffer with their Lord below;
>   They reign with Him above;
> Their profit and their joy to know
>   The mystery of His love."[13]

[12] Eph. ii. 15.   [13] Thomas Kelly.

But we must now turn to the second point which seems to be set forth in our text, and which is indeed already fully involved in the considerations that have been before us, viz., *Christ on the Cross the Representative of the entire human race:* " that He might reconcile them both in one body unto God." Such a statement could not have been penned had Jesus been only a national Saviour—a Saviour of the Jews only and not also of the Gentiles. But I wish to add to the testimony of the apostle in this place certain circumstances, connected with the crucifixion of our Lord, which seem to me to bear out his assumption that, at Calvary, Jesus was lifted up and suffered as the Representative of all men, the wide world over. I recall the fact, which I have already adverted to, that His death was consummated by the joint action of Jew and Gentile. This I am sure was no mere accident, but accorded with the divine purpose that the world's great Sacrifice should be offered up through the agency of both sections of the human race. And as those who took part in this great and awful transaction were virtually, though ignorantly, acting on behalf of our entire humanity, so may there be fulfilment by men of all nations and kingdoms, and peoples, and tongues, of the prophecy of penitence, that recognises the Saviour in the crucified One, " They shall look unto Him whom they have pierced : and they shall mourn for Him, as one mourneth for his only son, and shall be in bitterness for Him, as one that is in bitterness for his firstborn." [14] This of itself is enough to show that Christ hangs on the Cross as the Representative of all. But there are further and more direct evidences. Note the prayer prayed by our Saviour on the Cross: "Father,

[14] Zech. xii. 10.

forgive them; for they know not what they do." [15] This was uttered on behalf of those Roman soldiers who had nailed Him to the accursed tree. And thus, the very first petition that ascends from the mercy seat sprinkled with our Saviour's blood, is a prayer that attests the universal character of the offering that is through Him being presented on the altar of expiation. Need I recall to you another significant fact that belongs to this notable scene? the inscription above the Cross in Hebrew and Greek and Latin,[16] —the three representative languages of the age; an inscription which virtually proclaimed to all the true Israel of God in every corner of the earth, Behold your King! This may have been a mere whim of Pilate, designed to annoy those who had driven him to crucify Christ; but how often have divine purposes been served by human vagaries; and so it would not be at all surprising if the great truth, which is now before us, were designed to be attested involuntarily by this threefold inscription on the Cross. But we have proof even more emphatic than that which I have just adduced of the universally representative position which our Lord occupied at Calvary. His own language bears out the fact that He is the Redeemer of all men. For we have Him not only saying, " Many shall come from the east and the west, and shall sit down with Abraham, and Isaac, and Jacob, in the kingdom of heaven,"[17] a statement which testifies to the unrestricted application and effect of His gospel; but we have Him as well declaring, and that with most direct reference to His dying work: " And I, if I be lifted up from the earth, will

---

[15] Luke xxiii. 34.
[16] Luke xxiii. 38, John xix. 20.   [17] Mat. viii. 11.

draw all men unto Myself." [18] And the circumstances in which this latter statement was made impart to it a very special significance; for it was when the Greeks at the feast desired to see Him, and it was no doubt designed as an indication to them, and to all, that His approaching experience on the Cross was to be an experience endured on behalf of the whole human race. He was to be raised to this eminence in crucifixion that He might be able to cry to the children of men in every age, and in every land, " Look unto Me and be ye saved all the ends of the earth." [19] We may indeed say to every one, of whatever time or nation, This Saviour is your Saviour; He died for your sins; He represents on this Cross your case before your heavenly Father, and presents your Sacrifice; you have as much right to Him as any other one of the sons of men; behold Him here seeking to reconcile you unto God and His Father!

I am now brought in the last place, to the brief consideration of the point which I have just incidentally mentioned, viz., *The Cross as the medium of the reconciliation of man to God*, "that he might reconcile them ... through the Cross." Now note particularly that it is not the reconciliation of God to man, but the reconciliation of man to God that is here spoken of. It is not expiation then that is the prominent idea here, it is something else. No doubt, as we have already seen in former discourses, there must be first sacrifice for sin ere there can be acceptance of man by God, and the peace that follows thereupon. But, in the Cross, Christ did not merely present such Sacrifice, He also presented before the eyes and hearts

---

[18] John xii. 32.   [19] Isa. xlv. 22, see also above pp. 23, 24.

of men a picture that might well win them from their alienated condition and reconcile them to God. I think that the Divinity or Godhead of our Saviour is an essential of the gospel. If Christ had been only a creature, then we might have seen, in His Cross-bearing, what an awful thing sin is, that for its expiation there should have been required such a Sacrifice, but we would not have seen, how precious to God man is, that for the sake of man He should render such a Sacrifice—for the Sacrifice would not have been God's, but only that of the creature who had come to render it. And even had Christ been the highest archangel that stands before the throne, yet His suffering on the Cross would not have attested to us the love for us of the Father's heart—for it would not have been a suffering at the cost of the Father Himself. It might have set forth the justice, or the righteousness, but never the affection of God. It is however, the glory of the gospel that it sets forth the love of God, and that most manifestly in the Cross of Christ—and most manifestly in the Cross because He Who suffers there is God Himself, the Only-Begotten, Who dwelt in the bosom of the Father.[20] This is the cost to Himself at which God seeks to win us back. If we have been at variance with any one there is nothing which will more readily reconcile us again than some evident token and proof of that one's friendship and affection. Reconciliation can only take place on the basis of an assurance that no ill thoughts, no hard grudges, are harboured against us, and that, on the contrary, there is a yearning of the heart toward us, and a longing to be at peace and amity again. Now all this is supplied to man in

[20] John i. 18.

the Cross of Christ. It stands forth as pre-eminently a proof of the going out toward mankind of the heart of the heavenly Father. It is an evidence, which cannot be gainsaid, of the fact that He has nothing but the most loving and longing feelings toward us, and that it is His supreme desire that we should be no longer alienated from the experience of His grace and favour. He will do anything which it accords with His nature to do, in order to win us back—He will, He even *has* laid down His life that we may be assured of the yearning toward us of His soul. And it is when this assurance takes possession of us that we are reconciled to Him. Behold then, in the Cross, an efficient cause of such reconciliation! Whatever doubt you may have had as to the disposition of God relative to you, that doubt should disappear as you stand at Calvary. Every preacher of the gospel, having such a scene as this to set forth in the forefront of his message, may well exclaim: "We are ambassadors on behalf of Christ, as though God were entreating by us: we beseech you on behalf of Christ, be ye reconciled to God."[21] Surely when He Who has been wronged, Who has so great reason to seek judgment against us, shows so signally through the Cross that He is so far from being implacable, that He will do all that is required to secure for you His favour and His grace, you will not on your side be so implacable and full of enmity toward Him, that you will refuse and spurn His proffered peace.

> Be reconciled to God! see how His Heart
> Bleeds on the Cross with longing after thee,
> And lo! His words of grace the pale lips part:
> 'Oh sinner turn, and be at peace through Me!

[21] 2 Cor. v. 20.

I bear thy guilt, I take thy room and stead,
I bow beneath the falling of the rod,
And in My hands, and feet, and thorn-crowned head,
Behold the tokens of the love of God.'
His yearning soul is fainting to embrace
With arms of joy again His long-lost child,
To crown thy life with favour and with grace;
Oh sinner, turn to God, be reconciled.

V.
TRIUMPHING IN THE CROSS.

No tribunal so magnificent, no regal throne so glorious, no triumphal pomp so splendid, no chariot so sublime, as was that Cross upon which Christ overcame death and the devil—the prince of death, whom he utterly bruised under His feet.—CALVIN.

The Cross has so amply and lastingly satisfied the claims of inexorable justice, that all divine action now leans on the side of infinite clemency.—DR. DAVIES.

THE CROSS OF CHRIST

V.—Triumphing in the Cross.

Colossians II. 14, 15.—"Blotting out the handwriting of ordinances, that was against us, which was contrary to us, and took it out of the way, nailing it to His Cross: and having spoiled principalities and powers, He made a shew of them openly, triumphing over them in it."

In the last two discourses we have been considering that purpose of the Cross-endurance of Christ, which contemplates the bringing together again into amity and unity of God and man. Peace and reconciliation have been the great themes before us; the former flowing out of the latter as a river from its source, as a plant from its root. And the order of our investigation has been from effect to cause—a tracing backwards to the discovery of origins, and the unveiling of influences. The subject brought before us to-day by the words of our text calls for a continuation of the same process. We proceed still further backward, and retrace to a point still nearer its primal upspringing the course of that development of which the subsequent stages are the reconciliation and the peace which have already occupied our thoughts. For these would have been altogether impossible but for the great facts that find expression in our text—God and man would have remained for ever apart, the human would have been eternally alienated from the divine, the divine eternally severed from the human, had there not been that removal of barriers which is described in the verses we are to consider. All the longing of the heart of God, and all the searching of the minds of men, would have been futile had what is here called "the handwriting of ordinances" continued in force against us, and had the "principalities and powers" not been "spoiled." These are the essential pre-requisites to the establishment of renewed relationship between the heavenly Father and His erring children, and consequently to all the blessings and happiness which flow to man from this reinstalment into the position which had been lost.

The topics which have been already before us, relative to the reunion between the human and the divine, have rather dealt with the *subjective* elements that have gone to the accomplishment of that reunion—that is, with the elements existing within God and man: the disposition of God toward man, and the disposition of man toward God. But we are to-day led to the consideration of what we might call the *objective* elements which go to the accomplishment of this result—that is, the elements lying as it were outside of the parties who are to be reconciled and made at peace one with another: the abolition of obstacles that lie between them, the "taking away" of condemnatory accusations and sentences which stand on record against man, and the "spoiling" of supernatural agencies and intelligences that interfere with the gracious and loving purposes of God. Thus although the general theme is virtually still the same, viz., the bringing about of concord or harmony between those who have been sundered from one another, the region of our inquiry is altogether different, and the facts to be dwelt upon have little in common with those which have been already under review.

I propose to direct your attention to the following points which are set forth in our text, or may be fitly taken into account in connection with it, viz.:—

>1st. The obstacles which were removed by the Cross of Christ: (i.) "the handwriting of ordinances, that was against us, which was contrary to us," (ii.) "principalities and powers";
>
>2nd. The manner of the removal of these obstacles: (i.) "blotting out," "nailing .. to His Cross"; (ii.) "having spoiled ... He made a shew of them openly, triumphing over them in it."
>
>3rd. The notable and glorious results of this removal of obstacles that stood between man and God.

First then I ask you to consider with me *the obstacles which were removed by the Cross of Christ.* These, as I have already indicated, were twofold, "the handwriting of ordinances, that was against us, which was contrary to us," and "principalities and powers." And, as I have also already indicated, these were respectively barriers to the return of man to God, and thwarters of the gracious purposes of God to man. Let us endeavour to understand exactly what the nature of these obstacles is. The handwriting of ordinances may very well be that moral law which was traced by the divine finger on tablets of stone on the summit of Sinai, and, at least, there can be no doubt that the figure—if figure it be —is derived from the manner of the giving of the law on the sacred mount.[1] But a little consideration will shew that

[1] See Exod. xxxiv. 28; Deut. iv. 13.

to regard the phrase in our text as referring exclusively to the words of the ten commandments is to take quite an inadequate view of it. The decalogue—or ten commandments—does not by any means contain the whole moral law of God. It was given, as we have reason to believe, to meet the exigencies of a special condition—the condition of Israel just released from bondage, and particularly liable to certain sins. These sins are specially contemplated in the ten words issued from the mount of the law, and, as has been pointed out, the negative form of these commandments—the fact that they are all prohibitions, makes evident that they were framed to cope with a special case, to lay an arrest upon the commission of besetting forms of iniquity. In such circumstances it could not be expected that they would be exhaustive in character, covering the whole duty of man, and comprising every obligation which morally lies on man's shoulders. And, as a matter of fact, they are lacking in not a few important particulars. For, as has been pointed out, they form "only and really a code of relative duty of man to God and man to man, but personal obligation—that of man to himself—is omitted. There is no reference to health, sobriety, integrity, generosity, or truth—save in the matter of witness bearing in a court of law. And even in relation to relative duty, there is no injunction relative to marriage, or the duties of husband and wife, and none inculcating the duties of parents to children." [2] And there are other points which might be mentioned in which there is lack of completeness—so that we have to regard it as at most "but a fragment, and not in any true sense a summary of moral law." [3] And then we must remember

[2] Eadie, *Life by Dr Brown*, p. 162.   [3] *Ibid.*

that moral law had existence long before the promulgation of the commandments from Sinai, that, whether expressed or not, it sprang into being so soon as a moral creature was made, that it laid obligation upon angels before man was formed, and upon man before its specific terms were revealed. It is manifestly therefore wrong to suppose that "the handwriting of ordinances" is a phrase which refers only to the words that were given on Sinai, or that its application is even to be confined to those things—moral or ceremonial that were enforced upon, or at least laid down as requirements for, the chosen people. For the latter interpretation is at once too narrow and too wide—too narrow, in that it takes no account of many matters that must be considered as belonging to a right relation of man to God, and too wide in that it contemplates as being of universal and permanent character, duties that were only designed for a special nation, and for temporal observance. Hence it seems to me that the handwriting of ordinances is no less than the entire law of God, that law which, with greater or lesser distinctness, has been written on the consciences of all men, and written there as surely by the finger of God, as were the ten enactments delivered on Sinai. For every man's heart is a tablet on which at least traces of this writing can be found—only traces it may be, in that sin has obliterated much that was originally there, but such traces as, like the fragments of old inscriptions which we are wont to find amidst oriental ruins, attest a former entirety, and evidence the fact that, in his pristine state, man had the whole divine law engraven by the hand of his Creator on his inmost soul.

But this handwriting of ordinances, or "bond written in

ordinances," is described in our text as "against us," and, as "contrary to us," and the question arises, What is the meaning of this statement? A law that is broken becomes an accusation of the law-breaker, and if there be penalty attached to it that penalty becomes forthwith a sentence of condemnation. As originally conceived, law is neither for nor against any one. It is simply an expression of the requirements of moral order, and, in respect of those to whom it applies, is neutral or colourless. But if there be attached to it, on the one hand reward, and on the other hand penalty, then it becomes for or against one according as it is kept or violated. And it is in this manner that we must explain the phrase in our text. The law has become contrary to man or against him, because man has gone contrary to the law or against it. Hence the broken commandment has become at once an indictment of man, and a sentence of condemnation. And this is the first of the two obstacles lying between God and man that are spoken of in our text. For the condemnation, resulting from the accusation that is contained in the bond written in ordinances, shuts out man from the divine presence—the sentence is banishment from the face of God—exclusion from paradise—no more possibility of walking in that garden where the creature may meet and converse with his Creator. And in that man has, through his fall, lost the power of keeping the moral law, and is constantly transgressing against it, there is ever fresh accusation being heaped up against him, and, so to speak, a constantly widening gulf separating between him and his God.

Another obstacle to the union of the divine and the human is, however, made mention of in our text. For I take the phrase "principalities and powers" to indicate an element as surely hostile to man, and as certainly parting him from God, as that other which we have just considered. And the two barriers or obstacles are by no means unconnected. For, if the interpretation which I am about to give of the phrase before us be correct, then man's violation of the law of God was and is in great measure due to the baleful agency which the apostle here describes. It is of evil angels he is speaking, as I think, when he refers to "principalities and powers"; of those who kept not their first estate, and of him, exalted by his surpassing wickedness to that bad preeminence, who was and is head of the rebel host. I cannot suppose that, by such language as we have before us, the apostle is indicating some abstract impersonal influence and potency of evil existing in the universe, and inimical to our humanity. There are some who seem inclined to deny the existence of the Devil and his angels, and who would interpret such words as we are now considering in a sense that would avoid the necessity of thinking of any such individualities as having a place in the universe. But, in respect of this, I have just to remark that I do not believe that moral evil, or influences to moral evil, can exist apart from personality. There is an old theory, called the Manichean doctrine, which locates evil in matter and darkness, and good in spirit and light, and which divides the universe between two eternal principles that embody these opposing elements; but this is a pagan duality utterly opposed to Scriptural teaching, and especially opposed to it in that it makes moral evil an unintelligent substance, and not, as it really is, the voluntary act of a conscious and responsible being. But this is to strike at the very root of morality itself, and to make sin not a wrong-doing, but only a necessity of the existence of matter. We may safely then discard all opinions that would regard the "principalities and powers" spoken of in our text as mere abstract influences, tending to lead man to transgression. There must be personality behind all moral action be it good or bad, and so it is undoubtedly that army of wicked spirits who are described by the apostle in another place as "the world-rulers of this darkness .. the spiritual hosts of wickedness in the heavenly places,"[4] that is here referred to—that legion of malignant intelligences, whose head is called by our Lord "the prince of this world,"[5] and by the writer of the epistle to the Ephesians, "the prince of the power of the air."[6] These constitute the second barrier between the divine and the human which it was necessary for Christ to remove in order that the gracious purposes of God relative to man might be fulfilled. For, as at first they, or, at least, their impious head, contrived to thwart the design

---

[4] Eph. vi. 12.   [5] John xii. 21 ; &c.

[6] Eph. ii. 2. Commenting on this passage Eadie says in his *Commentary on the Epistle to the Ephesians*, "The *cosmos* of the New Testament is opposed to God, for it hates Christianity: the believer does not belong to it, for it is crucified to him and he to it. That same world may be an ideal sphere, comprehending all that is sinful in thought and pursuit—a region on the actual physical globe, but without geographical boundary—all that outfield which lies beyond the living church of Christ. And, like the material globe, this world of death-walkers has its own atmosphere, corresponding to it in character—an atmosphere in which it breathes and moves. All that animates it, gives it community of sentiment, contributes to sustain its life in death, and enables it to breathe and be, may be termed its atmosphere. Such an atmosphere belting a death-world, whose inhabitants are dead through their trespasses and sins, is really Satan's seat. His chosen abode is the dark nebulous zone which canopies such a region of spiritual mortality, close upon its inhabitants, ever near and ever active, unseen and yet real, unfelt and yet mighty."

of the Creator for the holiness and happiness of our race, so, ever since, have they been our adversaries; by their malignancy turning from us, or turning us from, the blessings which, in spiritual things, God would fain have bestowed upon us; shadowing the very light of heaven with their dark and baleful wings, arresting the lustre of the countenance of Jehovah, so that it has not shone on us, and, by the sufferance of Him Who rules over all, permitted, for a time, to prevail, even to the extent of seeming to thwart the plans of the Eternal, and to make of none effect, in so far as the vast majority of the human race were concerned, the whole of that preparatory dispensation that was set up and maintained in order to pave the way for the Desire of all nations—the Messiah of men.

But, having now sought to place before you some conceptions relative to the obstacles which were removed by the Cross of Christ, I ask your attention, in the second place, to *the manner of the removal of these obstacles*, as that is described in our text: viz., on the one hand, "blotting out" and "nailing to His Cross," and, on the other hand, "having spoiled ... He made a shew of them openly, triumphing over them in it." The first of these statements refers to the "bond written in ordinances," and we must remember, that this written bond was the law with its accusing and condemning indictment against our humanity. It is declared in the epistle to the Galatians that Jesus was "born under the law that He might redeem them which were under the law."[7] And this is a truth relative to the Saviour which applies equally to His life and His death. It makes His life one of servitude,

[7] Gal. iv. 5.

though He was the Son. But the important point before us is the aspect it imparts to His death. In consequence of that death being endured under the law it has a penal character imparted to it; it is a punishment, and that of a very signal nature. There falls upon the head of Christ in His Cross-bearing the condemnation which the law presents against our humanity, on Him the sentence is executed, by Him the full penalty is borne. For in estimating the measure of His sacrifice, and consequently its value as a paying of the penalty exacted by the broken law, we must not think of Him as we would think of an ordinary man—however innocent he might be—bearing such penalty; [8] but on the contrary, we must ever remember that, as has been noted, " The value of Christ's sacrifice was equal to His divine dignity, multiplied by His perfect obedience, multiplied by His infinite love, multiplied by suffering in body and soul,

---

[8] When, in accordance with the teaching of Scripture, we say, that our Saviour "bare sin" (Isa. liii. 12; Heb. ix. 28), and the punishment thereof (Isa. liii. 5; Rom. iv. 25; 1 Pet. iii. 18)—which is indeed, of necesssity, included in sin-bearing—we must carefully distinguish between what such statements mean, as applied to Him, and what they would mean, as applied to us. The bearing of sin and its punishment is a very different thing in the case of our fallen humanity from that which it is in the case of the sinless nature of our Lord. The same causes do not necessarily in every instance produce the same effects. If the light and heat of the sun fall upon a pestiferous swamp, they will call up therefrom deadly exhalations, and will foster foul and loathsome forms of life, both vegetable and animal; but if they fall upon ground that is clean and well tilled, they draw out the sweetest perfumes, entice the tender shoot from the soil, ripen the golden grain, and make to bloom the fairest of flowers. So must there be a very wide distinction between the issues of sin and its punishment, as we experience them, and their issues, as they were experienced by our immaculate Redeemer. In the first instance, finding in our fallen nature something on which to lay hold, they manifest themselves in corruption, remorse, and disease; but in the case of Christ no such features can be conceived of as presenting themselves. So that we can but say, He bore sin and its punishment in the only way, and as far as His sinless nature was capable of doing so. This, indeed, entailed on Him, suffering,

carried to the uttermost limit of what a sinless being could experience."[9] And when we look at His Cross-endurance in this light then we find in it that which suffices to support the apostle's statement : " Christ redeemed us from the curse (or the sentence) of the law, having become a curse for us : for it is written, Cursed is every one that hangeth on a tree."[10]

This then is the strong basis of fact on which is founded the statement of our text, that the bond written in ordinances has been blotted out, or washed away as with a sponge, so that its accusing and condemning indictment has become entirely obliterated, and that it has itself been nailed to the Cross, according to ancient custom, in sign of being cancelled, even when Christ was nailed to the Cross, and has died and disappeared with His death. It is thus for ever taken out of the way; it stands no longer as an obstacle between man and God, for the embargo laid upon us on account of our sin has been for ever removed ; there is no longer against us the divine sentence, Thou shalt not see My face and live ;[11] on the contrary, through Christ, we have " access unto the Father."[12] His Cross has become for us the ladder to heaven, even into the very presence of God ; the way without barrier that leads to the light of the divine countenance ; the upward

---

sorrow, and death, but nothing tainting His perfect purity, or shadowing His lustrous holiness. He was indeed treated *as if* He were corrupt, had anguish as keen *as if* it had sprung from remorse, and went down to death *as if* He were the victim of disease. In this way He bore our punishment, suffered in our room and stead, took our place. But we must ever remember that there is an "as if" in all of it; and that even through all His sin-bearing and penalty-enduring, He continued " holy, guileless, undefiled, and separate from sinners " (Heb. vii. 26).

[9] Bruce, *Humiliation of Christ*, p. 391.   [10] Gal. iii. 13.
[11] Exod. xxxiii. 20.   [12] Eph. ii. 18.

path to the new paradise, where no longer the cherubim with the flaming sword guard the gate, but the course is open and without impediment into the lustre of the love and grace of the Eternal One.

So much for the one obstacle referred to in our text, but what of the other? Does not that opposing host of evil spirits whose baleful influence so long darkened the firmament above us, and hid from man the light of heaven, still continue with its hostile ranks to bar the way of return to God? The response of the passage before us is clear and decided. These ill-omened "principalities and powers" have been spoiled by Christ on the Cross, and even there He has triumphed over them, so that, at His ascension—for such seems to be the reference of the words before us—He has been enabled to make a shew of them openly, to exhibit them as trophies of His victorious might, as ancient conquerors were wont, when they returned home from war, to make a spectacle of those whom they had subdued, by leading them in chains in the train of their triumphal procession. On the Cross Christ was fighting a battle as well as offering a sacrifice; He was contending against the great adversaries of men, He was combating the machinations of the enemies of the human race, and, when He bowed His head and gave up the ghost, His seeming defeat was a true triumph, for He had struck from the hands of our arch-opponent the main weapon of his war against us, in that He had made it impossible for him to accuse us before the presence of God, and to seek for sentence against us from divine justice. And then, when His work was finished, this great Victor from Edom, coming with His dyed garments from Bozrah, glorious in His apparel,

His raiment red with the sprinkled blood of His enemies,[13] ascended, to that heavenly region from which He had issued on His great enterprise, leading captivity captive,[14] and making a pageant for the eyes of angels and redeemed ones, in which the "principalities and powers," over whom He had obtained the victory, were openly set forth as defeated and spoiled. Such is the figure before us; and the great reality which corresponds thereto seems to be that, as a consequence of what transpired on the Cross of Christ, Satan and all his host were cast out of heaven, where up till that time they had entrance as the adversaries and accusers of men. For the same operation that opened to man the gate of approach to the divine presence, seems to have closed it for ever to demons and evil angels. At the ascension, the head of the rebel host and those who served under him were, as we read in the Book of Revelation, judged and cast out.[15] They could no longer walk among the sons of God, and present themselves before the Lord to bring accusations against the human race, as we find them doing in the Book of Job.[16] The entire firmament therefore between earth and heaven was, so to speak, cleared of their evil presence, so that "the prince of the power of the air" could no longer darken the atmosphere between man and God, nor spread the shadow of his poisonous wings over the human race. And now, his evil work must all be from beneath—figuratively speaking—

[13] Isa. lxiii. 1, 2.   [14] Ps. lxviii. 18.

[15] Rev. xii. 9-11—"*They overcame him because of the blood of the Lamb.*"

[16] Job i. 7-12; ii. 1-6; Even although in these descriptions we may have but poetical representations, the essential spiritual fact lying behind remains unaffected, and it is to this essential fact that reference is above made.

where he is permitted to have his will for a little until the second coming of Christ. At that second advent his influence with the human race—or, at least, with such of them as have accepted the Saviour, will be for ever destroyed, and the final deliverance of man from its noxious effects will take place; for, as has been well said, "we live in an atmosphere poisoned and impregnated with deadly elements; but a mighty purification of the air will be effected by Christ's coming." [17] The fact however now before us is but the first stage of this great deliverance, and what we are called upon to contemplate is the momentous truth that, through His Cross, Christ has swept the heavens above us clear of all evil agencies against us, driven forth those who would fain for ever have barred our way to God, and thus made easy for us that reconciliation with its consequent peace which is the highest blessing the love of God can bestow upon us, the greatest boon which any created being can obtain. The Cross was in fact a scene of triumph. Though there all the legions of wickedness seemed to have gathered in their serried ranks to fight against the Crucified One, and the whole heavens were darkened with their malignant and pestilential presence, yet, ere the battle was over, they were broken and scattered by a might greater than their own, and they fled discomfited from this sphere of unequal conflict. The shadow of their power passed away for ever from between earth and the throne of the Eternal—to this region they can never more return, so complete was the victory achieved by Him Who hung in apparent weakness on that

---

[17] Eadie, quoted by Braune, in *Commentary on Epistle to the Ephesians.*

Cross at Calvary. Those whom He has redeemed may now sing in gladness of heart as they look upon the spectacle which is presented to their eyes :—

> "Against Thee, fainting, wounded,
>   Nailed to the cursèd tree,
> The wrath of foes beat ruthless,
>   Like waves of raging sea.
> Yea, Death and Hell assailing,
>   By fury self-decoyed,
> Came, as if all-devouring,
>   There to be self-destroyed." [18]

The prophecy uttered of old time regarding Him has here, on this day of Cross-bearing, been fulfilled : " I have trodden the wine-press alone ; . . . yea, I trod them in Mine anger, and trampled them in My fury ; and their lifeblood is sprinkled upon My garments, and I have stained all My raiment. For the day of vengeance was in Mine heart, and the year of My redeemed is come." [19]

But, we must now turn to say a word or two, in the third and last place, regarding *the notable and glorious results of this removal of obstacles that stood between man and God.* These results are of two kinds, the one affecting the present position, the other affecting the future prospects of those who look, in faith, to Christ crucified. As for the present position of such, it follows, that since the law with its accusing and condemning indictment has been taken away—its accusation and its sentence blotted out, there is no longer aught against man. And is not this just what the apostle declares: "There is now no condemnation to them that are in Christ Jesus"?[20] The mouth of the adversary is shut,

---

[18] Robert Boyd, translated by MacGill.   [19] Isa. lxiii. 3, 4.
[20] Rom. viii. 1.

the voice calling for divine sentence against us is no longer heard. Already in Christ we have "tholed our assize," and borne our punishment, and the law has no second claim against us. This is the truth which our text testifies to every burdened, sin-conscious soul. There is no need that you endure what your Lord has endured for you. The price of your debt is paid, and, if you will, you may go free. The bond written in ordinances is a blank sheet, so far as you are concerned—the blood of Christ has wiped away the charge and expunged the sentence. And that same bond is now offered to you as a free pardon. Will you accept of it? It is from the gracious hand of Christ Himself, and you may have it " without money and without price." [21]

But there is another notable and glorious result of the removal of obstacles through the Cross; a result that flows especially from the fact that "principalities and powers" have there been destroyed. In respect of his whole future prospects the disciple of Christ has nothing to fear. No enemy can rob him of his participation in the triumph of Christ. "If God be for us, who can be against us?" [22] he may with confidence exclaim. "Greater is He that is with us than all those that be against us," he may with assurance assert. In Christ's Cross he has the guarantee of the entire future, for he stands in His strength Who has already vanquished all his foes. No wonder that he who writes at the beginning of the 8th chapter of the epistle to the Romans, "There is now no condemnation to them in Christ Jesus," should triumphantly exclaim at the end of it, when he has surveyed the majestic extent of the work of his Saviour: "Who shall separate us

[21] Isa. lv. 1.   [22] Rom. viii. 31.

from the love of Christ? shall tribulation, or anguish, or persecution, or famine, or nakedness, or peril, or sword?" that is, those things which evil "principalities and powers" may bring upon us. "Nay," he cries out, "in all these things we are more than conquerors through Him that loved us. For I am persuaded, that neither death, nor life, nor angels, nor principalities, nor things present, nor things to come, nor powers, nor height, nor depth, nor any other creature, shall be able to separate us from the love of God, which is in Christ Jesus our Lord." [23] This is the culmination of the truth that is before us. This assurance is the final end and aim of Christ's Cross. As such receive it. Let it be the stay of your heart in all life's vicissitudes, the staff of your journey to the end. Nothing in time or eternity need fill with fear those who, through Christ and in His Cross, are " more than conquerors."

[23] *Ibid* vv. 35-39.

VI.
PREACHING THE CROSS—FOOLISHNESS AND POWER.

Let us daily ask God to form around us an immense void, in which we shall see nothing but Him,—a profound silence, in which we shall hear nothing but Him! . . . Let us entreat Him to envelope us in His radiance and inspire us with the holy folly of His gospel . . . Let us not only pray without ceasing, but let us unceasingly watch, unceasingly strive; no means, no effort is too much to disengage us from the restraints of wordly wisdom, to make us die to that vain wisdom, and enable us to taste, in the bosom of God, the plenitude of truth and the plenitude of life.—VINET.

The Cross was but two pieces of dead wood; and a helpless, unresisting Man was nailed to it; yet it was mightier than the world, and triumphed, and will ever triumph over it."—ARCHDEACON HARE.

THE CROSS OF CHRIST.

VI.—PREACHING THE CROSS—FOOLISHNESS AND POWER.

1 Corinthians I. 18.—"*For the preaching of the Cross is to them that perish foolishness: but unto us which are saved it is the power of God.*"

In the course of these meditations on the Cross of Christ we have in succession considered, under various aspects, first, the spirit in which our Saviour suffered, and then, the purpose for which He laid down His life. This line of thought has brought before our minds His marvellous obedience—an obedience, the measure of which is no less than the distance between the Throne in Heaven and the Cross at Calvary; His unwearied and unmurmuring patience—a patience sustained even amidst the darkest experiences of Golgotha by the anticipation of the glory at last to be reached in the final triumph of His Kingdom; His gracious aim,—to expunge the accusations and the sentence of the law which were against us; and the issues which this momentous undertaking was designed to achieve, viz., reconciliation between God and man by the winning, through the manifestation of divine love, of the human heart, and consequent peace with all the blessings that flow therefrom, or are associated therewith, in time and in eternity. On this foundation of truth, which we have gradually been led to survey in the course of our inquiries, we must take our stand in now proceeding to contemplate the Cross, and to discourse upon it in a connection altogether different from that which we have up till the present borne to it. For, whereas, up to this point, we have been chiefly concerned with the meaning of the sufferings of Christ, we are now rather to direct our attention to their relation to the human race—the effects which they produce on the hearts and lives of men, the obstacles that lie in the way of their legitimate influence, the degree in which they may assert their power, and the absolute transformation or revolution in thought and in attitude toward Christ and toward God, which they may ultimately be the means of bringing about. These are themes which we could not have so advantageously considered had we not first laid the basis to which I have already referred; for the facts that are to be brought before us, and the statements which we must set forth in this connection, have their roots deep down in those great verities which it has been our aim to express and realise. And the more practical side of the subject to which we have now to turn derives all its strength and influence from the doctrinal foundation which has already been examined.

We begin this other branch of our inquiries with a passage which lays down, in most general form, the twofold and widely contrasting effect of the presentation of the Cross of Christ, through the ministry of the Word, before the minds of men. It is here asserted by Paul that, to use the exact rendering of the revised version, " The word of the Cross is to them that are perishing foolishness; but unto us which are being saved it is the power of God." The apostle had a special reason for writing in these terms to the Corinthian Church; but we need not detain ourselves on the present occasion by discussing that reason, as it will present itself for consideration in our next discourse, the text of which is in the preceding verse, and which will deal with some of the barriers in the way of the progress of the gospel. It will be also more appropriate to consider this reason at that stage, and meanwhile to take our text in its widest aspect, as presenting a striking and marvellous fact, viz., that the word, which sets forth the sufferings of Christ for man's salvation, may produce effects so widely different, that some will be hardened into contempt and antagonism, and others will be subdued and led to the recognition of the might of the love of God.

The Cross raised at Calvary was, figuratively speaking, designed to remain there so long as the world should last. The crucified One was to hang there before the eyes of all generations of men till the end of time. That scene was not to pass away till heaven and earth should pass away. And the manner in which it was to be kept before the vision of the human race was by witness-bearing. Our Saviour appointed His disciples to carry the news of His Cross to every nation under heaven.[1] The story of that event which took place at Golgotha was to be repeated in every tongue. The name of Him Who had suffered there was to be made known in all lands and in all ages. Of the apostle who penned the words of our text the risen Redeemer said, "He is a chosen vessel unto Me, to bear My name before the Gentiles and kings, and the children of Israel."[2] In a single phrase, through what Paul calls the "foolishness of preaching,"

[1] Luke xxiv. 46-48.   [2] Acts ix. 15.

Christ crucified was to be exhibited to the ends of the earth, and till time should be no more.

But there was to be one distinguishing feature about this preaching of the Cross which would ever differentiate it from all mere repetitions of historical fact which might be made by men: and this distinguishing feature it is which makes the scene at Calvary in every age practically an event of the passing day and not a mere reminiscence—a scene, so to speak, contemporaneous with each epoch of the world's annals, occurring in an everlasting NOW, and continuing, at least, so long as there is a soul to be saved. And this distinguishing feature is that every preacher of the Cross must himself present an example of the power of the Cross, so that out of the depths of his experience he may be able to say, "I speak that I do know, and testify that I have seen." To the eyes of faith Christ is indeed crucified to-day, and the voice of faith brings a message of that which has just transpired. Calvary exists in the heart of every one who is being saved; for indeed all the events of the gospel—from the cradle to the Cross, from the Cross to the Throne—lose their sequence to the soul that has possession of them, as outward aspects and pictures of great spiritual truths, and become coincident in that soul, in that the verities which they present to it are co-eternal facts, on the basis of which the life of faith is built. Hence we say that in and through the preaching of the Cross, when that preaching is from the heart of one who believes—and it can rightly come from no other—the tree raised at Calvary continues, and the crucified One remains, and the cry and invitation are still fitly echoed as from the lips of the divine Sufferer Himself: "Look unto Me, and be ye saved, all the ends of the earth." [3]

This setting forth of Christ and Him crucified, accompanied by this appeal to unredeemed and sinful men, is what the apostle means in our text by "the word of the Cross." And now we must consider the twofold aspect which this word presents—the twofold effect which it has on the minds of men :—

> 1st. To them that are perishing—"foolishness;"
> 2nd. To them that are being saved—"the power of God."

First, then, **the word of the Cross is to them that are perishing, "foolishness."** The heart of unbelief, and especially the heart that is hardened in unbelief, as well as the soul that is sunk in indifference, receives the message of the crucified Christ as an idle tale. It is to such at the most an historical fact, possessing, it may be, a certain amount of pathos, but destitute of all significance such as its preachers would attach to it, and, as a means to the end which they assert it serves, wholly inept and in every aspect absurd. It has been the lot of the word of the Cross to be thus derided from the very first; and it may be safely asserted that more than the teachers of any other system of religion the bearers of the news of Christ's sacrifice have been subjected to ridicule, to worldly-wise contempt, and to the pungent satire of irreligious wit. They have been named fanatics, ignorant enthusiasts, shallow dreamers, extravagant theorisers, weak dogmatists, and so forth; as if they carried off the palm for folly in the message which they bore. This attitude toward them is not the characteristic of any one age

[3] Isa. xlv. 22.

more than another: it began with those who taunted them for worshipping a crucified God, it has continued, with more or less marked emphasis, in every century since, and it is to be found in the present day in the gross sneer of the materialist and the lofty contempt of the agnostic. "The offence of the Cross"[4] —an offence, which we shall have opportunity of considering more fully on a future occasion—has ever existed, and seems likely to continue to exist, until that day when the Cross is made manifest to an assembled universe as the way to the Crown.

But we must endeavour to discover some of the grounds on which those who are perishing place their conclusion that the word of the Cross—and therefore the Cross itself as a means of salvation—is foolishness. These grounds we shall find in the objections which unbelief is wont to take against the gospel, and particularly against the Cross as the centre thereof. I make use of the latter expression of set purpose; for there are some who make pretence of receiving Christ, but will not have Christ crucified, who profess admiration for the example of His life and the wisdom of His teaching, but will not have His atoning death—to whom indeed this death bears little or no meaning, and to whom therefore the word of truth which has been promulgated in every age concerning it appears to be a word of folly.

There are many who hold that the word of the Cross is *foolish in its presuppositions*. The message which those bring, who with sincerity preach Christ crucified, is a message of extreme alarm. They represent the case of the human race as one of the utmost gravity—so grave as to necessitate not

[4] Gal. v. 11.

merely the descent to our earth of the Son of God, but to call for His offering up of Himself as a Sacrifice for the sake of man. Now it seems to not a few that this is an extravagant representation of the condition of our humanity. They cannot believe that there exists no power in man himself to retrace his steps to God, or that, if he gained the divine presence, his state is such that, without a sacrifice, or at least without such a sacrifice as lies beyond what he himself could render, he would not be acceptable. The charge against the gospel is that it seeks to cast terror into the hearts of men in order to constrain them to faith in the remedy it proposes, and that it makes use of a fiction for this purpose—the fiction of man's absolute and incurable sinfulness. It is therefore held up to ridicule as a mere figment, designed to capture the ignorant, and to frighten the weak.

But yet again, there are others to whom the word of the Cross is foolishness, because if the case of humanity be so serious as it represents, they hold that *the remedy provided is ludicrously inadequate to meet the necessity.* To these the simplicity of the gospel scheme is distasteful. They estimate the value or efficiency of a spiritual truth by its difficulty or complexity; and it seems to them utterly absurd to imagine that a plan, which in respect of its most important features even a child can understand, should be the divine plan for saving the human race. If there had been in the word of the Cross, as that word may be presented in the first instance to the sinful soul for its redemption, something of a much more subtle quality than on the surface appears, it would have commended itself to this class of mind, and, in proportion to the trouble which its apprehension might occasion, would seem to such fit for the end in view; but they cannot endure its exceeding transparency, its perfect plainness of meaning, its translucence. So accustomed have they become to consider that alone profound which is perplexing, that alone deep which is turbid and muddy, that the story of the Cross seems to them but a foolish legend, fit only for the infancy of the race. They forget indeed that the very first condition of an effectual remedy for man should be its fitness to meet the capacity of all without exception—and that therefore this ground, on which they exclaim against the gospel, is the very ground on which it may be most effectually defended as a divine plan; for it is the glory of God "who willeth that all men should be saved, and come to a knowledge of the truth,"[5] that He has made the means for the attainment of this so plain that, whilst perhaps the pride of the wise and the prudent may hide His plan from them, it is nevertheless revealed unto babes. [6]

But I remark once more that there are some who say that the word of the Cross is *foolish because of the view which it necessitates of the divine requirements for human salvation.* There can be no doubt that it represents God as accepting sacrifice for sin. But these unbelievers declare that it is absurd to suppose that God should be so implacable as to call for the sacrifice of His Son, ere granting to our humanity the boon of pardon. Hence the Cross seems to them but the central figure of an idle tale; and the scriptural assertion that "apart from shedding of blood there is no remission,"[7] appears in their eyes but the hollow nightmare of a system of sacrifice that finds its culmination in the offering up of the

[5] 1 Tim. ii. 4. [6] Mat. xi. 25. [7] Heb. ix 22.

Christian Saviour. I do not stay to note the misrepresentation which this charge of folly against the gospel constantly makes—in that it speaks of God *demanding* a sacrifice and ignores the far more important side of God *offering* a sacrifice —that is, pictures the divine Father as implacably requiring the shedding of blood, and has nothing to say of the divine Son, freely offering Himself for the sake of man; presents a travesty of God's justice, and hides from view God's love—I say, I do not stay to note this; for it seems enough here to say that this indictment of foolishness against the word of the Cross has, at its basis, a partial human conception of the character of God, which it sets up as more profoundly wise than that which Revelation from beginning to end consistently places before us. And it seems to me that, if in anything, surely in this, "the wisdom of this world is foolishness with God."[8]

But I remark yet again, and finally here, that others assert that the word of the Cross is *foolish because it announces great and glorious results which cannot possibly issue from it.* Christians who accept this word are often looked upon as amiable enthusiasts who are being led captive by an absurd hallucination. Their anticipations of a future life are laughed at, their declarations as to their personal experiences in this present life are treated as illusions, and their belief in the regenerative possibilities of the Cross of Christ, in the application of its power to individual life, or to society, is spoken of as visionary and Utopian. For such effects cannot, it is asserted, spring from such a cause; it is not merely that the means are inadequate, it is that there is no relation whatever

[8] 1 Cor. iii. 19.

between means and end in the case, that the one does not contain anything which can lead to the other, that there is utter lack of causal relation—or, to put it otherwise, no living principle in the seed that can bring forth such fruit. Hence again, to those that are perishing, the word of the Cross is foolishness, and those who carry it are either designing deceivers or are self-deceived. Such is the verdict of the world when confronted with the scene on Calvary.

But now we turn to the other side of the subject, for our text speaks to us of a far different effect, and declares, Second, **"the word of the Cross" is to them "that are being saved the power of God."** It may seem at first sight that the antithesis presented in our text is somewhat faulty. When we are told that, to those who are perishing, the preaching of Christ crucified is *foolishness*, we should have expected immediately to read that, to those who are being saved, it is *wisdom*, instead of which we are told that it is "the power of God." There is, however, a correspondence here, implied if not expressed. That which men deride they regard as weak, and so, conversely, they consider the Cross as folly because they do not believe that it can accomplish the purpose for which it is proclaimed to men. That is, when Christ crucified is placed before them they see only an inept and feeble picture, and it is to them a matter of astonishment that any one should find in it a forceful influence, or moral and spiritual efficacy. But this is precisely what those who are being saved have, through their own experience, discovered in it, and what they can testify regarding it to their fellow-men.

For the word of the Cross is first of all *powerful over the human heart,* and this because it sets forth so affectingly the proof of amazing self-sacrificing love. Even those who have never felt the thrill of looking at the Cross with faith have sometimes been forced to confess the pathetic character of the scene of which it is the centre. One of the most notable of the unbelieving French philosophers—Diderot—declared that the most accomplished of the authors of his period, (and that was a period in which the highest literature of France flourished,) could not with all their genius construct a tale so sublime, so ingenious, so full of moving power, and fitted to exercise such a sway over the minds of men for so many centuries as the simple story of the Cross.⁹ But it is not simply of power of this kind that I speak when I say that the saved have experience thereof in their own hearts—it is not mere artistic influence or pathetic virtue such as might arise from fiction as well as from fact; it is living power, the power to mould and change, the power to purify, the power to exalt, the power to constrain to loyalty and fidelity to Him Who suffered for us, and the power to endure for His sake as He endured for ours. All this in its manifold forms the Cross exercises over the hearts of those who have in faith yielded themselves to its sacred influence.

Now in order to estimate the character of this power we might bring it into contrast with the power which the world is wont to exert, for thereby we shall find that it is unique, that is, is without parallel, and that, in comparison with it,

---

⁹ Denis Diderot (B 1713—D 1784), one of the projectors, and the chief editor of the great French *Encyclopédie,* a work noted for the promulgation of Sceptical opinions concerning religion. The statement referred to was made in a company of *Encyclopédistes,* comprising many of the most eminent literary and philosophical writers of France.

what men are wont to call force is but weakness, and their greatest strength but a feeble effort. There are two points of view from which this may be shown, viz., that which the apostle must have occupied when he wrote our text, and that which we now occupy with the advantage of nineteen centuries' history of gospel progress behind us. Let us first look at it from Paul's point of view. He only knew the power of the gospel by noting its influence on the individual heart and life, but he saw that it was already effecting what no world-power could accomplish. For it is a well known fact that material forces, however great, are impotent to influence the heart; they cannot essentially change the mind, or remould the disposition, they cannot captivate and hold the purer affections, nor indeed constrain to alteration of ideas. The combined power of the ages cannot make an individual or a people different morally or spiritually from what they choose to be. You may fetter the hands by world-power but you cannot fetter the heart, you may restrain the limbs but you cannot restrain the mind, you may imprison the body but you cannot imprison the soul. In the sphere of these things the power of the world is vain. But not so the power of God through the Cross. It acts in an altogether different way from that in which these other forces, of which I speak, go to work. It lays hold of a man within, it throws its influence over his heart, it achieves its conquests in his soul. It acts upon him not in an arbitrary, external fashion, but, planting its germ within his soul, grows from the centre outwards, expanding, developing, and shaping, in a free, spontaneous and entirely voluntary manner. And thereby it works out a change which exalts, ennobles, purifies, and finally glorifies the individual on whom its sacred influence is exerted.

But as I have already indicated we can look at this power from a point of view which Paul could not occupy. We can contemplate its effects, and doing so find that it is not only powerful over the heart, but as a consequence thereof, is *powerful over the life.* We have nearly nineteen centuries of evidence to its character, and we can see as even he could not how it is truly the power of God to those who are being saved. For what a change has through it been wrought upon the world! Take your stand at Golgotha, and let your eyes scan the vista of the world's history as it developes from the point at which the Cross is reared. Look first around you at the condition of things contemporaneous with the crucifixion of Christ. Is not the whole creation groaning and travailing in pain together? Amongst the Jews you find formalism, bigotry, fanaticism, and intense worldliness. Amongst the Greeks perplexity, groping in darkness, vain endeavours by wisdom to lay hold of the skirts of God. Amongst the Romans licentiousness, cruelty, hatred, deficiency of natural affection, and contempt of family ties. From subject nations there arise the groans of the oppressed, the cries of those trampled down under wars of aggression, the imprecations of the wronged and the enslaved, and the savage shout of retaliation. And on the horizon all around are peoples and races living in Cimmerian darkness, dwelling in the shadow of death and without one single ray of spiritual light. [10] But as you pass away from the contemplation of the world in the aspect which it presented when the great event at Calvary was enacted and glance down into the future, the scene is gradu-

[10] See Farrar, *The Early Days of Christianity*, Book I.

ally yet surely changed. First there appears a small band whose faith contrasts with surrounding perplexity and doubt, whose joy is an antithesis to the world's sorrow, whose purity rebukes the world's sin, whose love shines reproachfully on the world's hatred, whose hope puts to shame the world's fear, and who, notwithstanding persecution, and spoliation, and hardship, and torture, and even death itself, maintain unshaken their faith, yea even glory in tribulations and count all things of no value that they may be found in Christ.[11] What is it upholds them in their constancy, their fidelity, their courage, immovable as a rock? It is the power of God through the Cross. But look still further down the course of history and a wider development meets your eyes. The little leaven is leavening the whole lump. Vice is gradually giving place to virtue, ignorance to knowledge, unbelief to faith, cruelty to compassion, selfishness to charity, oppression to freedom, perplexity to assurance, formalism to sincerity, in short, chaos to order. Kings and emperors, alike with the meanest of their subjects, bend the knee to, and acknowledge the sceptre of, the Prince of peace. What has produced this marvellous transformation? Again the reply must be given, The power of God through the Cross of Christ. Look down to still later times, and, although here and there dark shadows of superstition, and ignorance, and priestcraft, obscure what might otherwise be uniformly fair, yet, on the whole what a wondrous change from the first picture is presented to the eyes! The world is in great part Christianised; at least a high and pure type of civilization flows around

---

[11] As exemplified in the great Apostle of the Gentiles; Acts xx. 24; Phil. iii. 8.

the earth and appears, more or less, in almost every land. Institutions, the noblest and most beneficial, flourish on every soil. The distressed are relieved, the enslaved are set free, the down-trodden are rescued, the weak are protected. There is manifested a higher tone of morality; a wider charity; a more emphatic assertion of the common brotherhood of man; a more perfect realisation of our duty towards nations lying in unbelief and ignorance; the initiation and carrying on of manifold missionary and benevolent enterprises; and the exhibition of self-denial, brotherly-kindness, Christian courage, temperance, patience, godliness, truth, honesty, and other graces, amongst those with whom, in past ages, selfishness, malignity, cowardice, licentiousness, profanity, ignorance, and deception had prevailed. And again we ask, What has produced this change? and again we must reply, The power of God in the Cross of Christ; the subtle influence and inspiration flowing forth from that scene on Calvary to which so often of late our thoughts have been turned. What kingdom or conqueror in the earth, what form of world-power, ever has produced, or ever could produce a change approaching to this? Do not these results manifest the fact that what, to unbelief, is foolishness and weakness, is really unique wisdom and unique power?

And this power is a power to those who are "being saved." There is a significant meaning in the form in which it is here spoken of. It is no force at all to unbelief. It is a strange thing, but true, that, efficient as this force seems to be, it may be resisted, and is resisted and thwarted by every one who looks not in faith at the Cross of Christ. Unique though this divine Might may be, it is not omnipotent in the sphere of human will—that is, it cannot change, and so save us, in spite of ourselves. Do not be surprised then that the practical lesson of this part of our text should be, that you submit yourself to the influence of the Cross. An appeal to your will is not inconsistent with the fact that the might of Christ crucified is greater than that which any other possesses. For it is the might of Love; and the manner of Love is, not to compel, but to win. Let Him therefore gain the victory over you and lead captive your hearts. The power of His Cross will transform you, that same power will lead you through all the experience of your earthly life, making you safe amidst all its trials, and temptations, and sorrows; and when you have crossed the Jordan, which you shall do, upheld in its swellings by the same might, then shall the power of the Cross be finally made manifest, in the unlocking to you of the gates of the Celestial City, and the bringing of you into the midst of the happy company that there ascribe honour and glory, dominion and power to the Lamb that was slain. [12]

[12] Rev. iv. 10, 11; v. 12, 13.

VII.
MAKING VOID THE CROSS.

By so much the more are we inwardly foolish, by how much we strive to seem outwardly wise.

. . . .

By how much the more man seeth the light of grace, by so much the more he disdaineth the light of nature.—GREGORY THE GREAT.

Christianity has a might of its own, by which dejected, suffering humanity is re-elevated from time to time, and when we grant it this power, it is raised above all philosophy, and needs no support therefrom.—GOETHE.

THE CROSS OF CHRIST.

VII.—MAKING VOID THE CROSS.

1. Corinthians I. 17.—"To preach the Gospel, not with wisdom of words, lest the Cross of Christ should be made of none effect."

I indicated in last discourse that the apostle Paul had a special reason for writing to the members of the Corinthian Church in the terms then under our consideration. It had been in accord with his experience that the word of the Cross, was to them that are perishing, foolishness, but to them that were being saved, the power of God. But the same facts that had led him to this conclusion had as well conducted him to certain decisions both as to the manner and as to the matter of gospel-preaching. And now to-day, when we are brought into contact by our text with these decisions, it is fitting that we should direct attention to the grounds on which he was constrained to come to them. We have reason to believe that when he first visited Corinth, for the purpose of proclaiming the truth, he was deeply depressed in spirit, was filled with an acute sense of his own inefficiency as a preacher of the word, and was greatly humbled by an experience of comparative failure through which he had just passed. This experience had occurred at Athens, to which city he had come in high hopes of achieving a great triumph in the cause of his

Master. It was the centre of the intellectual activity of his times, the supreme seat of learning, and the meeting place of philosophers from all parts of the world. This may have had an effect upon the apostle, of which perhaps at the time he was scarcely conscious, for it must be admitted that he did not speak with his wonted directness and simplicity, but, as it were, suiting himself to his audience, addressed their minds rather than their hearts, and brought to bear upon them his native powers of reasoning and his knowledge of their own literature and customs. But, as we find from the historical account, his well-prepared disquisition had but little success. The philosophers were moved to ridicule rather than impressed; they derided both the manner and the matter of his discourse; whilst others, too polite to turn his well-meant efforts into food for their mirth, but no doubt looking upon him as some harmless dreamer, with studious courtesy, dismissed him with that indefinite promise, which is the usual empty excuse of those who would get rid of a subject with regard to which they feel indifferent, "We will hear thee again of this matter." Now, when we examine the address which met with this discouraging reception, we find that it seems in its character a most powerful intellectual argument —an argument most skilfully adapted, as we would suppose, to the circumstances in which it was delivered, and the audience to which it was spoken. It is indeed one of the most acutely reasoned of all the appeals which, in behalf of his divine Master, Paul ever presented. We cannot sufficiently admire the adroit manner in which he seeks to lay hold of the sympathies of his hearers, grasps the one element of truth which they seemed to have in common with himself, and on this builds up argument and appeal, exhortation and warning. He also lays under contribution their own literature, supporting the truth of his assertions by a quotation from one of their poets, and the whole of his language, from beginning to end, was couched in that style of eloquence which seemed no doubt to him most suitable to the culture and the intellectual standing of those to whom he spoke. But despite all this, the fruits of that supreme effort were sadly disappointing. Indeed we may say that its immediate effects were no less than lamentable, and, but for the conversion of Dionysius, Damaris, and one or two others, the whole stay of the apostle in Athens, of which this notable speech was the climax, would have been a miserable failure.[1] On account of this want of success, Paul entered with fear and trembling the city of Corinth. He was never more conscious of his own weakness than when he set foot on its busy streets and mingled with its gay and gain-pursuing crowds. So completely had his recent experience cast him down, that, as he himself virtually declares, he determined to attach no " importance to anything that human means, human eloquence, and human wisdom could furnish toward procuring an entrance for the publication of the divine word. . . . He had experienced that it availed him nothing to become a Greek to the Greeks in his mode of exhibiting divine truths, where the heart was not open to his preaching by a sense of spiritual wants."[2] Hence he made the resolution not to come, as he remarks in the beginning of the second chapter, " with excellency of speech or of wisdom, proclaiming . . the mystery

---

[1] Act xvii. 32-34.
[2] Neander, *History of the Planting and Training of the Christian Church*, Book III. Chap. vi.

of God." [3] He was determined "to trust solely to the simple and unadorned grandeur of his message, and to the outpouring of the spirit by which he was sure it would be accompanied. There was indeed," as has been noted, " a wisdom in his words, but it was not the wisdom of this world, nor the kind of wisdom after which the Greeks sought." [4] It was the wisdom which contented itself with simple enunciation of the great central truth of the gospel, which perceived that therein lay that which was best adapted for every condition of unbelief, for the polished philosopher as well as for the rude barbarian, for the quick-witted merchant of Achaia as well as for the dull peasant of Lycaonia. It was the wisdom of God which fits in most perfectly to every phase of human want, and beyond which, on the first presentation of the truth to the ignorant or doubting there is no need to go. On this alone would he place reliance in his proclamation of the gospel at Corinth ; " For," as he writes, " I determined not to know anything among you, save Jesus Christ, and Him Crucified. And I was with you in weakness, and in fear, and in much trembling. And my speech and my preaching were not in persuasive words of wisdom, but in demonstration of the Spirit and of power : that your faith should not stand in the wisdom of men, but in the power of God." [5] And, already in the words to-day before us, he justifies his formation of, and acting upon, this resolution ; for even had not his experience at Athens led him inevitably to it, he must, on reflection, have reverted to the simplicity and directness of a divinely commissioned ambassador, since, as he here records, Christ

[3] 1 Cor. ii. 1.
[4] Farrar, *The Life and Work of St. Paul*, Book VIII. Chap. xxvii.
[5] 1 Cor. ii. 2-5.

sent him "to preach the gospel: not in wisdom of words, lest the Cross of Christ should be made void."

The general theme which is brought before us by this passage is the neutralising of the legitimate effect of the Cross of Christ by the manner of its presentation. And whilst undoubtedly the reference of the apostle in our text and its surroundings is confined to one particular instance or example of this, nevertheless we may from the starting point thus afforded proceed to the consideration of other obstacles by which the forth-going of the power of the Cross is hindered, for the "wisdom of words," not merely in the sense which we must attach to that phrase in this place, but in other forms as well, has often stood between Christ Crucified and those to whom His gospel has been sent, making the latter as if it were but a pleasing theory or a poetic picture, instead of a divine plan for the rescue from sin and sorrow of the human soul. Accordingly I propose to call your attention to these two topics that legitimately connect themselves with our text:

> 1st. The Cross has sometimes been made void through "wisdom of words" by being presented as if it stood merely on the level of human philosophies and speculations;
>
> 2nd. The Cross has sometimes been made void through "wisdom of words" by being hidden behind them instead of being set forth by them.

First then, in strictest accordance with the meaning of Paul when he wrote the passage before us, I remark that the Cross has sometimes been made void, or of none effect through "wisdom of words," *by being presented as if it stood merely on the level of human philosophies and speculations.* It was characteristic of the Cultured of the apostle's time that they were much engaged in the pursuit of philosophical learning. There were many schemes and theories abroad which occupied attention; and discussion on which, was esteemed the mark of intelligent and thoughtful minds. There were Sophists, and Stoics, and Epicureans, and Pythagoreans; followers of Socrates or of his interpreter, Plato, of Aristotle and of Philo; multitudes who, having broken with the old Pagan faiths, were engaged in that vain quest, to which in another passage the apostle refers, when he says, "the world through its wisdom knew not God." [6] Such inquirers, with more or less earnestness, set themselves to determine which of the opinions and speculations of their wise men were most worthy of credit; in which philosophical school they might most reasonably enrol themselves; which afforded the best key to the meaning of life, and suggested the best rules for the conduct of it. Many of them pursued these studies not with any hope or desire of reaching truth at all, but simply as an agreeable and not unexciting pastime, and as a relief to the intolerable ennui or "weariness of life" which characterised the period. Now it will be perceived that in these circumstances it was distinctly dangerous, and likely to be damaging to the credibility of the gospel, to present it in terms borrowed from the language of, or to set it forth associated with conceptions that had their origin in, these contending schools of philosophy. For what would those already familiar with such terms and conceptions conclude regarding it, save that it was just another of the current conjectures and conceits which men were inventing, in their guesses after verity, and was only to be judged on the

[6] 1 Cor. i. 21.

principles which might be applied to any theory or surmise of human authority? And the utmost which these might be expected to say regarding the facts of the Cross of Christ, when placed before them after this fashion, was just that which was said by the Athenian philosophers: "He seemeth to be a setter forth of strange gods," and "We will hear thee concerning this matter yet again."[7] The fact is that to robe the simple story of the Cross in the jargon of philosophy is to degrade it from the great and grave dignity of a divine proclamation to the mean level of human speculation. It is to introduce it into that arena of conflict in which the guesses of men contend with each other, and seek by subtlety to outwit and triumph over each other—in which, more frequently than otherwise, words that are utterly empty take the place of facts, and the victory is gained by that which is least practical and most abstruse. Now the truths that centre in, and emanate from the Cross of Christ belong to a region altogether different from that in which these trifles exist. They constitute the supreme message of revelation; and it is as incumbent to place them before men in their purity and simplicity as it is necessary to publish any royal proclamation or command in the language in which it has been dictated. Who would have the foolishness to seek to convey in words of philosophical wisdom tidings of pardon and acceptance to condemned rebels, or to set forth in terms of abstruse speculation news of amnesty granted by a sovereign to traitorous subjects? Would it not indeed be itself traitorous to take such liberty with a message emanating from such a source? And how much more traitorous to venture so to present the word

[7] Acts xvii. 18, 32.

of the gospel that it shall be stripped of the marks of its divine origin, and assume the aspect of a merely earthly conceit!

But the main point is, that when so placed before the minds of men it is almost certain to be made void or of none effect. Reason for this has been already given in what I have just said, in that the very manner of presentation at the outset tends to cast suspicion upon it, and to prejudice against it, those to whom it is offered. But there is another reason which connects itself with this same aspect of the subject before us, and which should be taken into account at this stage. The gospel of Christ is meant to be urged rather upon the emotions than upon the intellect, and to make its appeal rather to the heart than to the head. The Cross was raised at Calvary that it might captivate the human race, win their love, and subdue their enmity. It is not so much the reasoning faculty that is addressed, or rather that should be addressed, when the story of our Saviour's sufferings is presented, as the affections—not indeed that the former is, or ever can be, neglected, but that it occupies not a primary but a secondary place. When, however, in the sense in which the terms are used in our text, the message of the Cross is set forth in "wisdom of words," it is, of necessity, only directed to the understanding. Philosophy has little to do with the heart of man; it rather discourages that which lies in the sphere of feeling, speaks of it as being untrustworthy in the search for truth, and questions if it should not rather be suppressed, or, at least, altogether left out of account, in matters that concern man's well-being. Hence there is no channel through which the story of the

Cross may with less advantage be conveyed than that which is here warned against and repudiated by the apostle. It is about as unfit for the conveyance of it as mathematical formulæ are for the expression of sentiments of friendship and love. No wonder then, that when through "wisdom of words," attempt is made to tell the story of redeeming love to men, miserable failure is the result. The reward apt to be reaped by those who make the trial is more likely to be derision and mockery than the joy of leading lost souls to the heavenly Father. And this is the case in every age, when men, in seeking to set forth Christ Crucified, forsake the simplicity of the gospel message and deck their preaching in the language of the schools. They may awaken admiration, in the minds of those to whom they speak, by their intellectual acumen, but they leave their hearts as hard as the nether millstone, and they are no more likely to lead men to salvation than one would be who should address fine philosophical reflections to a drowning man and neglect to cast him a rope.

But I pass on to note now, in the second place here, that the Cross of Christ has sometimes been made void, or of none effect, through "wisdom of words," *by being hidden behind them instead of being set forth by them.* There is a strong, uncompromising aspect about many of the truths that find their foundation in the sufferings of the Saviour, somewhat ill-suited by their realism, it may be, to content fastidious minds, and too pronounced in their sharp contrasts of light and shade to fit into human canons of taste. And it has frequently been the endeavour of gospel preachers to tone down these glaring opposites, to produce a more pleasing picture of the Cross-bearing of our Lord, and to meet half-way the dainty and dilettante religionists, to whom the facts of human sinfulness and of divine sacrifice as presented in the gospels are not too well-pleasing. There is an emasculation of the great and notable verities that stand over against each other in all their bold and awful antithesis at Golgotha. A little light is thrown upon the dark side of the picture—man is not so evil after all; and a little shadow is thrown upon the bright side of the picture—this is the manifestation of divine love, but not of love in sacrifice; and thus there is produced a nearer approach to artistic chiaroscuro than the crude facts of the Crucifixion as placed before us in the gospel narratives present, and the strikingly contrasting spiritual truths relating to human nature and divine intervention, which the apostles establish thereon, display. But all this blending is but a hiding of the Cross, for it is brought about at the expense of the truth as to man's need and the truth as to God's mercy. Whatever tends to minimise the great verities relative to these, tends as well to make the Cross void or of none effect. Make man feel that he is not so bad after all, nor in so perilous a case; lead him to think that God's love is not so great as it really is, and that it has not stooped so far as to die for him, and you place an obstacle in his way and turn him aside from the acceptance of his Lord. Is not this what that "wisdom of words" which seeks to explain away Calvary, and to thrust it in the background as the means of human redemption, is constantly doing? All the fine poetic frenzies with which we are familiar in the works and utterances of a certain class who cannot bring themselves to believe in sacrifice for salvation, who shrink from the doctrine of blood-bought redemption

—a doctrine so uncompromisingly proclaimed in every page of the New Testament—all this, is no other than a preaching of the gospel which makes the Cross void; a preaching of a gospel which is no gospel at all; a draping of the scene on Calvary after such a fashion that, from being the centre of human hope, it becomes only a centre of mystery, a perplexing and inexplicable event.

But I have to remark that there are other ways of making futile the presentation of Christ Crucified, besides that which I have just mentioned, by hiding through the supposed "wisdom of words" the Cross and Him Who suffers on it. There are methods of doing this, of which even those are sometimes guilty who do not deny the propitiatory sacrifice, and do not doubt the need of that sacrifice by man. Lord Macaulay relates in his article on Southey's edition of the Pilgrim's Progress that upon one occasion James the Second sat for his portrait to Varelst the famous flower painter. When the picture was completed the king appeared in the midst of a bower of sunflowers and tulips so beautifully painted that the attention of the spectators was completely drawn away from the central figure, and all who looked, thought it was merely a fine flower-piece.[8] I fear that there are some word painters who thus, whilst professing to set forth, really obscure the Cross of Christ. They wreathe it in so many flowers of rhetoric, overload it with such gorgeous illustration, that it is actually buried beneath them. And in the present day they who do this, whilst much to blame, are yet sorely tempted. For the tendency on the part of the majority of those who read and those who hear is to esteem more highly the manner of the

[8] Macaulay's Essays (Lond. 1886) p. 133.

presentation of the truth than the truth itself. Those who thirst for popularity can only gain it by that word-wisdom which exalts the expression far above the value of the thing expressed. The Cross is constantly being hid by its exponents behind their presentations or professed presentations of it. How many there are who shrink from the bare truth; who must have everything mellowed and toned down; the Cross placed before them in beautiful song, or in language that shall not make it too obtrusively realistic. Now all this is wrong. We are covering the throbbing of the heart of God with ornament that veils it from our sight. A religious worship which is smothered beneath a gorgeous ritual seems to me not half so bad as religious truth buried beneath a mass of fine verbiage. I would rather have Romanism, with all its ceremonial,—detrimental though I think it to be to sincerity and simplicity in the service of God,—than some forms of present-day Protestantism, that cover the great verities of the Christian faith with such a halo of the poetic, or with such a glare of the sensational, that nought can be seen save the artistic, or the dramatic frame or envelope in which it is assumed the truth lies concealed. Of what avail these when it comes to be the question of the saving of a soul? You who are led to be in earnest about truth will want nothing but the simple Cross set before you in the plainest of language, and the great verities of the Cross stated in all their magnificent proportions without adornment or admixture of human element. The "wisdom of words" is of small account to perishing men, it is the *wisdom of facts* that they want; and they are impatient of all that lumber and trumpery which the unrenewed, or the frivolous Christian, who forgets the

MAKING VOID THE CROSS.

essential worth of his faith, is wont to esteem so highly. When a man has got a grip of solid truth he does not care to see it tricked out and draped, as if it were a poetic dream, or a pleasing fiction. It is too precious to him to be thus treated, the realisation of it too valuable to be thus trifled with, and the revelation of it too soul-absorbing to be obscured from his sight at any time by the artificialities of a mere word-wisdom. For he realises that just in proportion as such human elements prevail, the Cross, and all that pertains to it is weakened in effect.

Now this is one of the most subtle and insidious influences that are in the present day at work sapping and undermining the legitimate power of the Cross. Coming in the guise of a friend to commend it, it is really an enemy to distract from it. It is, in truth, Satan appearing as an angel of light, and appearing in such a mask, that he seems to deceive even the very elect. There are many proofs of it to the observant mind, but the most evident is that to which I have already referred, viz., the tendency to esteem more highly the forms of the message of the gospel than the facts of that message; and its corollary, that we find even Christians, and, much more, those who are still in unbelief, speaking far more about the messengers than about Him from Whom the message comes. These are days in which people wait for human instrumentalities that they may be revived and quickened, and think little of the Cross when it is set forth in connection with the ordinary means of grace. One would imagine that the effects are to be expected not from that Cross itself but from some secondary source. This was the idea of the Corinthians to whom the apostle wrote. They ran after the ministry of

Apollos or of Cephas or of Paul, splitting up into sections, each of which declared for one or other of these favourite preachers, as if the gospel depended upon any of them; and the apostle has to bring them to their senses by asking them in a verse that precedes our text " Is Christ divided? was Paul crucified for you? or were ye baptized into the name of Paul?" [9]

The Cross, and the Cross alone, is the means of salvation; not the eloquence of this or that preacher; not the adornment in which the truth may be presented; not the "wisdom of words" on which so many pride themselves; not anything else, however interesting or striking or beautiful it may be, —but the Cross, and only the Cross. Let it be realised by you in all its grand simplicity, and it cannot fail to influence your hearts—it will not prove void, will not be found to be of none effect. It no more needs any admixture of human wisdom than the sun needs the aid of a flickering rushlight to show forth its brilliancy. For its message to us requires no commentary, and no commendation from the lips of men. Its wonderfulness as a revelation, and its noble simplicity, make it both attractive and easily apprehended.

> " Inscribed upon the Cross we see,
>   In shining letters, ' God is love ;'
>   He bears our sins upon the tree,
>   He brings us mercy from above." [10]

Let this love, this substitutionary and sacrificial element, and this pardon-securing efficacy, which are so lustrously set forth at Calvary, be but realised, and surely the prayer will spontaneously rise from every sin-laden soul:

[9] 1 Cor. i. 10-13; see also Chap. iii. 3-5.
[10] Thomas Kelly.

"Lord of my heart, by Thy last cry,
 Let not Thy blood on earth be spent—
Lo, at Thy feet I fainting lie,
 Mine eyes upon Thy wounds are bent,
Upon Thy streaming wounds my weary eyes
Wait liked the parchéd earth on April skies.

Wash me, and dry these bitter tears,—
 O let my heart no further roam,
'Tis Thine by vows, and hopes, and fears,
 Long since—O call Thy wanderer home;
To that dear home, safe in Thy wounded side,
Where only broken hearts their sin and shame may hide." 11

11 John Keble.

VIII.
THE OFFENCE OF THE CROSS.

I began then to turn my mind to the Holy Scriptures, that I might see what they were. But behold, I see a thing not understood by the proud, nor laid open to children, in mien lowly, in issue lofty, and veiled with mysteries; and I was not such as could enter into it, or stoop my neck to follow its steps. For not as I now speak, did I feel when I turned to those Scriptures; but they seemed to me undignified, in comparison with Ciceronian dignity; for my swelling pride shrunk from their humble method, nor could my sharp wit penetrate their depths. Yet were they such as would grow up in a little one. But I disdained to be a little one; and swoln with arrogance, took myself to be a great one.—AUGUSTINE.

THE CROSS OF CHRIST.

VIII.—THE OFFENCE OF THE CROSS.

Galatians V. 11.—"The Offence of the Cross."

In last discourse I turned your attention to certain obstacles that stand in the way of the legitimate influence of the sufferings of the Lord Jesus Christ upon the hearts and lives of men—obstacles arising from the manner of the presentation of the gospel, and so detrimental to its progress, as to make the Cross of Christ of none effect. These, as I indicated, are, of course, mainly due to shortcoming on the part of the preachers of the faith, who, trusting to "the wisdom of words," lead their hearers away from the great central verities of Christianity to vain questions of philosophy, or hide from them the main features of the truth by emphasising things less important, or present it in such a framework that attention is distracted from the chief fact and figure—the Cross and the Crucified One—and absorbed by the merely incidental surroundings in which these are placed.

But there are other obstacles to the legitimate effect of the sufferings of Christ upon the minds and conduct of those to whom they are presented—hindrances that partly connect themselves with the manner of the presentation, and partly with the prejudices and prepossessions existing in the hearts of men, and so warping their understanding as to give them a bias against the simple truths which form the essence of the gospel. The text we have to-day before us refers specially to one class of these obstacles, and suggests other species of them that have existed and still exist as insuperable barriers to the cause of Christ, or, at least, barriers not easily removed. The meaning of the phrase "the offence of the Cross" is the offence which is occasioned by its proclamation, the repugnance to it which is sometimes created when it is set forth as the sole means of salvation, the antipathy with which it is viewed by a certain type of religious sentiment—an antipathy so great that, in place of being received as the cardinal means of redemption, it is regarded as a stumbling-block and resented as an insult.

The historical circumstances which led to the writing of this epistle to the Galatian church bring clearly out the specific nature of the offence to which the apostle here refers. Into the region from which the members of this church had been gathered Paul had come during one of his missionary journeys, and, by the simple preaching of the story of the Cross, had won many hearts and blessed many lives. And, as was his wont in his work as a pioneer of the gospel, he had founded Christian communities, which were excavated by him from the very depths of Paganism. Of the welfare of these, as of the welfare of all the churches which he was the means of raising, he was fondly careful and jealous. He bore them ever on his mind, made constant mention of them in his prayers, longed to hear of them and from them, and yearned after them as his spiritual children.[1] It was accordingly with no small degree of concern that he learned that,

---
[1] E.g. Phil. i. 3, 4; Col. i. 3, 4; 1 Thes. i. 2, 3.

following upon his ministry amongst them, there had entered into their midst Judaizing teachers, who insisted that the Cross was not sufficient for salvation, and that there must be, in addition, circumcision, and the keeping of the Jewish law. These teachers had not only made havoc in the Galatian church, but they had accomplished this by a misrepresentation of the character of Paul. They represented him as inconsistently preaching circumcision in some places and not in others, and hence, as being, according to their view, alternately lax and strict, so that he might secure success by suiting himself to circumstances.[2] And this is the charge which Paul indignantly denies and disproves in the verse from which we take our text. It was a well known fact that he was hated and persecuted by the Jews wherever he went. But this could not have been so if he had cunningly accommodated himself to them. Jewish Christians would at least have viewed him with favour. Such, however, was not the case, so that he can triumphantly refute the calumny to which he has been subjected, by referring to the fact that he continues to be obnoxious to that class: "If I yet," he says, "preach circumcision, why do I yet suffer persecution?" Is it not evident that "the offence of the Cross" would have "ceased" had he been complaisant in this particular toward the Jews, and that they would no longer have hounded him from place to place as they did, would no longer have interfered with his labours, and would no longer have constantly tracked his footsteps in order to thwart or undo his work? But "the offence of the Cross" had not ceased, it was still a stumblingblock to the Jews, hence they continued to be

[2] See Chap i. 7; iii. 1; iv. 9; vi. 12.

embittered against him, continued to malign him, and continued to do all in their power to bring to nought his influence amongst those to whom he had preached the truth.

Now these historical facts bring before us one class of obstacles to the legitimate effect of the Cross of Christ, and, in addition to this one class, there are other two to which I wish, in the present discourse, to direct your attention, and which are specially suggested by the terms of our text. Let us consider in succession :

> 1st. "The offence of the Cross" arising from its presentation as the complete means of salvation ;
>
> 2nd. "The offence of the Cross" arising from the obloquy and shame which befell the Crucified One ;
>
> 3rd. "The offence of the Cross" arising from its significance as a symbol and prophecy of sacrifice.

First, then, we have to consider "*the offence of the Cross*" *arising from its presentation as the complete means of salvation.* This, as we have already seen, is the particular offence which is referred to in our text. It is manifest that those who took exception, from the Jewish standpoint, to the preaching of the apostle, would have had little to say against him, or it, if he had insisted upon the external rites and obligations that belonged to the Mosaic law. Their objection was not to the Cross, but to the Cross as the *sole* means of redemption. They could not believe in, nor receive, a salvation in the procurement of which they themselves had no part. It was incredible to them that, through the death of Christ on the Cross, and through that alone, without any effort of their own, they could be made acceptable to God. They thought it incumbent upon themselves to commend themselves in the divine sight by their own righteousness, and to justify themselves before God by their own obedience. Their training, no doubt, conduced to this idea, for one effect of the Jewish faith, as it was then mistakenly apprehended, was to create the spirit of Pharisaism, and to foster religious pride.[3] At the same time, the offence which they took at the absolutely free offer of salvation through the Cross, though nurtured by their previous religious surroundings, springs as well from a deep-rooted prejudice in human nature; so that, although the specific form of this offence does not appear amongst those who have not been imbued with Jewish ideas, yet the spiritual pride out of which it grows is common to our humanity, and makes the Cross a stumblingblock to many besides the children of Abraham. This "offence of the Cross" has, by no means, even yet ceased. When from an enlightened standpoint, we look at the condition, and at the helplessness of our human nature, we wonder that spiritual pride can exist at all in the breast of man. But, just as natural pride takes up its abode in many a wretched lodging, so is it with this religious loftiness. The gift of free grace, the offer of unconditional redemption through the sufferings of our Saviour, is even yet scandalous in the eyes of many. They will not stoop to accept on these terms; it is derogatory to their dignity, it offends their self-esteem, and it presupposes an abject moral and spiritual weakness which they are by no means willing to admit. Hence, like the Jews of old, they would make certain additions to the requirements for salvation, they would introduce certain elements of their own

[3] See Rom. x. 2, 3.

devising and their own out-working. I am persuaded that, far more extensively than we have any conception of, this stubborn reluctance to accept God's gift in all its freedom lies at the root of the failure of the Cross to affect the hearts of unbelievers. This is shown by the estimation in which not a few profess to hold those who rely upon Christ Crucified for the redemption of their souls. They regard them as mean-spirited, as lacking in the more robust qualities of humanity, as altogether poor creatures who take refuge under the shadow of the Cross from evils which they might meet and overcome by their own stamina. And all this, and the like class of ideas, with which we are still to the present day quite familiar, are plain indications of the continued existence of that offence of the Cross, which took exception to it as the sole means of salvation, and of which we find the earliest examples in the Pharisaic Jew.

Now, regarding this particular barrier which comes between men and the acceptance of Christ, I have to remark, *first*, that the idea of supplementing the Cross is derogatory to the merit and glory of Him Who suffered thereon. It questions the completeness of His work, it makes the Human a partner with the Divine in the great enterprise of redemption, and it casts suspicion on Christ's power to save. There is at once an invasion of His prerogative when any human device is added to His Cross-bearing as an adjunct for the procurement of salvation. And there is nothing more certain than that He will have no co-worker in this matter—nothing more certain than that He can have no colleague or coadjutor in the redeeming of the souls of men. He has "trodden the wine-press alone," and the glory of this He will not give to another.[4] It is in vain that we come to Him for redemption if we do not approach empty-handed. And I care not whether they be Pharisaic deeds of self-righteousness, or ritualistic acts of self-commendation in the sight of God, or Romanistic presentations of good works, one and all of these form an actual disqualification for the reception of the benefits of the Cross, as well as an unworthy slur upon Him Who has there wrought out, to its last item, the entire enterprise of redeeming our humanity. Who will dare to compete with, or even to pretend to aid Him in this vast work which He has undertaken for our sakes? Who will bring forward their little tapers, or kindle their little altar fires, to add to the efficiency of the light and heat of the Sun of Righteousness in this noon-day of gospel grace? Who will stretch forth the hand to touch the ark of safety lest the sacrifice on the mercy seat should be overthrown or should fail? Is not all this supplementing of the Cross impious and sacrilegious and blasphemous? But worse still, Is it not the interposing of a barrier that makes the Cross of none effect? There is but one way of coming to Christ on Calvary, and that a way recognised most widely by every true section of the church of Christ—not even excepting the church of Rome, which has had the tendency to go furthest astray on this very point; for in that church too the song is sung:

> " Not the labour of my hands
> Can fulfil Thy law's demands :
> Could my zeal no respite know,
> Could my tears for ever flow,
> All for sin could not atone ;
> Thou must save, and Thou alone.

[4] Isa. lxiii. 3 ; xlii. 8 ; xlviii. 11.

> Nothing in my hand I bring,
> Simply to Thy Cross I cling;
> Naked, come to Thee for dress;
> Helpless, look to Thee for grace;
> Foul, I to the fountain fly;
> Wash me, Saviour! or I die." [5]

But a *second* remark I have to make regarding this particular obstacle which the pride of man is prone to place between the Cross of Christ and himself, is that it is an invasion of that freedom which Christ has, through the Cross, secured to all who accept Him. It is an attempt to impose upon man, who has entered into "the liberty of the glory of the children of God"[6] a fresh yoke of bondage, to enslave him again after he has become a son of the heavenly Father. Bunyan represents it graphically when he tells how Worldly Wiseman of the town of Carnal Policy turned Christian out of the narrow way of the Cross to the house of Legality, and how this aberrant path was up a mountain which, as Christian advanced, threatened to fall on and crush him, amidst lightning flashes and thunder peals from the summit.[7] A true and vivid illustration of the sad exchange which men make when they forsake the peace of the liberty of the gospel for the terrors of the yoke of the law. And, in respect of this, Calvin has well said: "If men lay upon our shoulders an unjust burden it may be borne; but if they endeavour to bring our conscience into bondage, we must resist valiantly, even to death. If men be permitted to bind our consciences, we shall be deprived of an invaluable blessing, and an insult will be, at the same time, offered to Christ, the Author of our

---

[5] Augustus Toplady.
[6] Rom. viii. 21, compare Gal. v. 1 and Chap. iv.
[7] *Pilgrim's Progress*, Part i.

THE OFFENCE OF THE CROSS. 147

freedom."[8] We have need to guard ourselves against the insidious attempts of those who, being offended at the liberty wherewith Christ makes His people free, endeavour to undermine that boon, and to lead us into captivity again. Even the liberties of our native land should not be of more account to us than this liberty of the gospel, this freedom purchased for us by the blood shed on the Cross at Calvary. Of all places in the world's history that is the place of emancipation, there the fetters were shattered and the chains broken once and for ever. This is

> "A Liberty unsung
> By poets, and by senators unpraised,
> Which monarchs cannot grant, nor all the powers
> Of Earth and Hell confederate take away:
> A Liberty which persecution, fraud,
> Oppression, prisons, have no power to bind,
> Which whoso tastes can be enslaved no more.
> 'Tis Liberty of Heart, derived from Heaven,
> Bought with HIS blood Who gave it to mankind,
> And sealed with the same token."[9]

"With freedom did Christ set us free: stand fast, therefore, and be not entangled again with the yoke of bondage."[10]

But we must now pass on, in the second place, to consider *"the offence of the Cross" arising from the obloquy and shame which befell the Crucified One.* In a former discourse I pointed out the nature and the degree of the opprobrium which attached to such a death as our Lord endured, and sought to show how intense an element it was in His humiliation.[11] Now, somewhat of this opprobrium descended upon those who accepted Him as their Saviour. They were taunted as the

---

[8] Quoted by the Editor in Schmoller's *Commentary on the Epistle to the Galatians,* p. 131.
[9] Cowper, *The Task,* Book v. 538-547.
[10] Gal. v. 1. [11] See above, pp. 35-38.

disciples of the accursed, as the worshippers of a crucified God, as the followers of one who had suffered as a malefactor. They were the objects of derision and contempt both to Jews and Gentiles—to the former on account of their abhorrence of every one who had been put to death after the manner in which Christ had suffered, and to the latter because of the apparent absurdity of professing faith in a person who had been subjected to the indignity of a slave's execution. In these circumstances it is not to be wondered at that many should discover an offence in the Cross, that it should be to the Jews a stumblingblock, and to the Greeks foolishness;[12] and that, simply on account of this, there was a barrier presented to the minds of some which they could not overcome. It no doubt seemed to such, madness that the preachers of the gospel should place this in the forefront of their message. Many perhaps thought that it would have been wiser to dwell more on the undoubtedly miraculous works which Jesus had performed, and upon the words of far-reaching wisdom which He had uttered, and less on that catastrophe which seemed to close His ministry. But the true preachers of the evangel knew that this was not so, and that, however men might deride and despise, the great fact that carried with it hope and help to sinful men was the Cross and its dying Victim. And those who were to be saved by this Cross must therefore of necessity "go forth unto Him" Who suffered thereon, following Him by the *Via Dolorosa* without the city, and "without the camp, bearing His reproach."[13] Blessed were they who could disregard this "offence of the Cross," and, despite all the shame they had

[12] 1 Cor. i. 18.   [13] Heb. xiii. 13.

THE OFFENCE OF THE CROSS. 149

to bear, freely took their places beneath the accursed tree, that, looking in faith, they might find redemption through the shed blood of the Crucified One.[14]

Now there can be no doubt that this particular aspect of "the offence of the Cross" has no existence in these later times—the obloquy has all passed away, Christianity has, by its very history, glorified that around which there existed at first so much degradation and shame. The Cross is now the emblem of highest honour. And yet there is an offence of the Cross of a similar nature to that which is now before us still existing, and, in some measure, impeding its progress in the hearts of men. We have even yet when we go to Christ to issue from the camp bearing His reproach. There is the sneer of the hard worldling, and the contempt of the self-applauding man of false culture, and the ridicule of the narrower scientists, and the cold scorn of the assuming philosophers, and the bitter gibe of the callous indifferentists, to endure by all who sincerely accept the Cross as the means of salvation. There are still multitudes who assume a superiority to their fellow men in respect of intellectual acumen and wit, and who, from their exalted pinnacle of wisdom, look down upon such as profess to have found safety in Christ, and a yet greater multitude who, caring for none of these things, load with censure, and twit with sarcasm such as are serious in respect of the faith, and especially such as have their faces turned towards Calvary. Now whilst all this lies comparatively lightly upon the genuine Christian, and he cares little what others may think of his attitude toward the truths of the Gospel, yet it forms a real stumbling-block to

[14] See Mat. xi. 6.

not a few who, but for it, might be found among the ranks of those who trust in Christ. There are always many who would rather have the praise of men than the favour of God; many who would rather that their fellows should think them to be in the right, than be in the right in defiance of the opinion of those around them. Opinion is a tyranny from which multitudes have not yet shaken themselves free. If their surroundings are anti-Christian they have not the courage to set their faces against those around them, even after conviction has come to their minds. They are cowards at heart, for they will rather be unfaithful to their deepest impulses, than break with irreligious companions, or run the gauntlet of derision and satire, which idle and foolish lips are ready to rain upon them. What a wretched thing is this! that man, for fear of the reproach of some fellow-weakling in the world, should shrink from declaring for Him Who bore the very climax of reproach for his sake; should hesitate to accept as a Saviour, because of the cheap sneer of a sinner like himself, Him Who, that He might bring him redemption, "endured the cross, despising the shame." [15] Let every one who is entangled by this "offence of the Cross" have the courage to step forth from a bondage which is infinitely more degrading in reality than the suffering of all the scorn of men is degrading in appearance. Whatever reproach you may bear for the name of Christ, count it your highest honour to have incurred it—it is the brightest crown you can wear.

> "Ashamed of Jesus! sooner far
> Let evening blush to own a star;

[15] Heb. xii. 2.

> He sheds the beams of light divine
> O'er this benighted soul of mine.
> Ashamed of Jesus! just as soon
> Let midnight be ashamed of noon;
> 'Tis midnight with my soul till He,
> Bright Morning Star, bid darkness flee.
>
> Ashamed of Jesus! that dear Friend
> On whom my hopes of heaven depend!
> No; when I blush, be this my shame,
> That I not more revere His Name. [16]

But now in the last place we must hasten to consider "*the offence of the Cross* *arising from its significance as a symbol and prophecy of sacrifice.*" There can be no doubt that Jesus meant something real when he said "If any man would come after Me, let him deny himself, and take up his cross, and follow Me,"[17] as also when at another time he added "Whosoever doth not bear his own cross, and come after Me, cannot be My disciple."[18] And in both of these instances we must interpret the word cross, by our Lord's own endurance thereof. It is something in our lives corresponding to that in His. And His Cross is therefore a prophecy and symbol of what the Christian may expect and should be prepared to render. This is a truth not to be refined away, nor to be ignored in the Christian system. The freedom of the Gospel does not mean that man shall have no sacrifice to make for Christ and His cause; it means that man shall have no sacrifice to make for himself. But it is not for a moment to be supposed that those who are redeemed by the blood of Christ may, without incurring blame, selfishly shut themselves up to the enjoyment of their salvation, and bear

---

[16] Joseph Grigg and Benjamin Francis.   [17] Mat. xvi. 24.
[18] Luke xiv. 27.

no cross in their Christ-following through the world. All religion is related to duty, should be indeed the mainspring of obligation, and the Christian religion is no exception to this general truth. If a man says that he accepts Christ and Him crucified, and cannot point to a single sacrifice which he has made for his faith, cannot distinguish any cross which he has borne for the sake of the Master, then his experience gives the lie to his profession. There is no use in shutting the eyes to the fact that our Saviour has made this cross-bearing a touchstone or test of our Christianity. His language is too exact to admit of any ambiguity—we cannot, and dare not explain it away—it is explicit to the very verge we might almost say of harshness: "let him deny himself, and take up his cross," and except he do this "he cannot be My disciple." There must be, on behalf of Christ, by every genuine disciple, sacrifice of some kind or another—of time, of talent, of ease, of money, of that which is held dear, and the parting from which involves real deprivation.

Now it cannot be denied that this is "the offence of the Cross" in the eyes of very many. They are not prepared to give up things that are cherished by them for the sake of Christ; to crucify certain enjoyments of this world, it may be, that are inconsistent with the faith, or to abandon certain enterprises that cannot be carried on in harmony with it, or to contribute freely of their time, talents, and substance, to further the cause of the Master. They would like to have the salvation, but they cannot bear the cross; they would fain possess the privileges but they shrink from the duties; they desire the blessings but they detest the obligations. And on this account "the offence of the Cross" stands as an

THE OFFENCE OF THE CROSS. 153

insuperable barrier in their way, it is an obstacle they cannot overcome, an impediment they cannot get beyond. And it is to be feared that there are many professing Christians who are not real Christians on this account. They would follow Christ, but they will not take up the cross. They foolishly imagine that the words "I desire mercy and not sacrifice"[19] mean that God will bestow mercy upon those who will not, even after they have accepted His salvation, do aught to show their gratitude. It is a miserable fallacy, and it is sending thousands to perdition.

You must conquer this "offence of the Cross" if you would have the benefit of the Cross. It is the most perniciously defrauding stumblingblock of all. I pray you not to imagine that this requirement of cross-bearing means the taking away with the one hand what has been given by the other. It rather means that you have come to realise the amazing character of the love of God exhibited to you in and through Christ Jesus, and that you are ready to accord to Him, out of a returning love, any sacrifice which He may call upon you to render; it means that the Cross at Calvary has had so overwhelming an effect upon you that you esteem all other crosses as nothing in comparison therewith, and are ready, out of gratitude therefor, to bear them should such be your lot, or should opportunity offer. May it be yours to obtain the victory over this and every other "offence of the Cross"; to rise superior to every barrier that would come between you and the Crucified One; and thus to accept of His Cross as your complete salvation, to bear joyfully whatever of reproach it may bring you, to carry cheerfully whatever

[19] Hosea vi. 6; Mat. ix. 13.

burden it may lay upon your shoulders, and render willingly whatever sacrifice it may require you to give. Then, indeed, will "the offence of the Cross" cease for you, you will glory in it, and glory as well in every opportunity presented to you of showing forth your admiration, your devotion, and your love to Him Who died upon it that you might live.

IX.
THE ENEMIES OF THE CROSS.

How shall ye help this man who knows himself,
That he must love and would be loved again,
Yet, owning his own love that proveth Christ,
Rejecteth Christ through very need of Him?
The lamp o'erswims with oil, the stomach flags
Loaded with nurture, and that man's soul dies.
                              —Robert Browning.

THE CROSS OF CHRIST.

IX.—THE ENEMIES OF THE CROSS.

Philippians III. 18.—"The Enemies of the Cross of Christ."

In last discourse the theme which occupied our attention was "the offence of the Cross"; *i.e.*, the offence created in the minds of men by the presentation of those truths of which the Cross is the centre. And, as we then saw, the world of unbelief is chiefly scandalised by these three elements—*first*, the doctrines that set forth the Crucified Redeemer as the sole Procurer of salvation for man—doctrines that sorely wound human pride, and cast down the natural Pharisaism of the heart; *second*, the reproach that has often to be borne for the sake of, and as it were with Christ, by those who profess faith in Him; and, *finally*, the suffering which may be entailed upon the Christian through the sacrifices which he is called upon to render, and of which the Cross itself is both a symbol and a prophecy. Against these things there rise up all the prejudices and the prepossessions of the unregenerate heart—vanity, self-love, epicureanism—in short, the entire host of those interests that seem to be vested in human nature ere it is renewed by the Divine Spirit. And these quicken into active hostility to the verities of the faith such as are animated by them, so that they may well be described on account of their attitude toward Christianity as "the enemies of the Cross of Christ."

But, antagonistic as these are, it is not to such that the apostle is referring in the passage from which we take our text, and, fitly as they might be designated by the terms of our text, it is not here designed to apply to them. The fact is that Paul has altogether a different class in view—not those who are outside the limits of the Christian profession, but those who, at least, pretend to be followers of the Lord Jesus. Strange as it may seem, there were in his time, and it is to be feared that there are still, some who go by the name of Christian, of whom it must nevertheless be affirmed that they are "enemies of the Cross"—enemies all the more dangerous, in that they are within the camp of Christianity, and fitted to work all the greater evil against the sacred influence and power of the Cross, in that they profess to have accepted as their Saviour the Crucified One, and to be washed and made clean by the blood that was shed on Calvary. The context leaves us in no doubt as to the class which the apostle has in his mind. For he is enjoining the disciples in Philippi to a course of conduct becoming such as have embraced the faith, and, whilst he sets before them example, he considers it necessary as well to present them with warning. Not all who say that they are believers are to be followed in the way of Christian life; there are not a few whose conduct belies their profession; for says the apostle, "Many walk, of whom I told you often, and now tell you even weeping, that they are the enemies of the Cross of Christ." And it is made evident, both from the description of the character of these unfaithful ones which succeeds, and from the language that goes before our text, that they were such as were unwilling to be partakers with Christ in His sufferings, such as were not ready to crucify the flesh with its affections and lusts, and were not seeking that the world might be crucified unto them, and they unto the world. They were rather those of whom the solemn words are written in the epistle to the Hebrews, who, by their evil lives, and by their disregard of the testimony of the Cross to the enormity of sin, going on, unchecked by their faith, in the way of self-indulgence, shamelessness, and worldliness, thereby crucify to themselves the Son of God afresh, and put Him to an open shame.[1] As has been pointedly said, "So far from the Cross of Christ proving itself to be 'the power of God' in their reformation of heart and life, it was actually used by them as a plea for transgression. In their unbridled licentiousness they continued in sin, that, as they supposed, grace might abound. They thus, by their practice contradicted, denied, and put to scorn the very significance of the Saviour's death. So far from knowing 'the fellowship of His sufferings, being conformed to His death,' they did despite unto the Cross in its saving and sanctifying energy, and made the religion, whose symbol it is, not only a cause of ruin to themselves, but also a scandal to the world."[2] No wonder that Paul calls them "the enemies of the Cross of Christ."

It is to their character, and to the injury which therefrom accrues to the Christian faith, that we must direct attention to-day. For by their attitude and action they form the most formidable of obstacles to the legitimate effect of the sufferings of Christ, they obscure and becloud His Cross, interfering sadly with the issues of its presentation to the world, indeed, we may say that they are more injurious to the spread of

[1] Heb. vi. 6.
[2] Dr Hutchison, *Lectures on the Epistle to the Philippians*, pp. 205, 206.

Christianity than are all the machinations of those who are openly arrayed against the truth, and that therefore, despite their professed allegiance to the Saviour, the startling words of our text more fitly apply to them than they do to such as, being offended by the doctrines of the Cross, deride the Divine Sufferer, blaspheme His holy Name, and deny the power of His finished Work.

In three particulars, the character of "the enemies of the Cross of Christ" is set forth in the passage which follows upon our text; and it will be well for us to pursue the line of thought which is thereby laid down, as by this means the antithesis between what these so-called disciples are, and what according to their profession they should be, will be most clearly brought out, and the nature of the harm which they do to the faith will be most clearly realised. In place of displaying those characteristics that befit the following of the Lord Jesus, they are noted for:

    1st. Self-indulgence; "whose god is the belly";

    2nd. Obliquity; "whose glory is in their shame"; and

    3rd. Worldliness; "Who mind earthly things."[3]

The first characteristic then of the enemies of the Cross of Christ is *self-indulgence*; "whose god is the belly." The form in which this is expressed indicates a certain amount of contempt for the ignoble nature of the worship to which these are addicted. They are such as were sunk in the depths of coarse, self-pampering, and materialistic pursuits; such as were akin to the groveller into whose mouth the poet Euripides puts the words: "I sacrifice to no one but myself; not to

[3] v. 19.

the gods, but to this my belly, the greatest of the gods; for to eat and drink each day is the god for the wise man." [4] There is surely no more contemptible creature under the sun than the man who cannot restrain his appetite, and who levels himself with the brute that he may worship this idol.

But the particular phrase before us is rather designed, I think, to be suggestive of a general characteristic—such as that which I have named, than to limit our attention to a special type thereof. It is the broad fact of self-indulgence that is emphasised by the placing before us of one of the grossest and most repulsive shapes it assumes. And the point that requires specially to be noted is that self-indulgence in all the variety of its aspects is so out of harmony with Christianity that, whoever is enslaved by it, whoever makes it the chief object of life—the idol before which homage is payed, must be declared to be an enemy of the Cross of Christ. For the great principle exemplified in, and designed to be impressed upon our humanity by the Cross of Christ, stands at the opposite pole from this vice. It is the crucifying of self that is placed before us in our Saviour's example on Calvary. And whilst the crucifying of the Son of God is the effective means of our salvation, yet it is not to be supposed that the scene which sets this forth, and upon which the eyes of faith must ever be fixed, is only to be viewed as redemptive, or that it can be separated from the rest of Christ's ministry amongst men as if it had no exemplary character—that is, nothing calling for imitation as well as for trust. On the contrary, the whole teaching of Christ, whilst elevating the Cross as the means of salvation, as well insists upon its pre-

[4] Euripides, *Cyclops*, quoted by Dr Hutchison, *supra* p. 207.

eminence as a pattern to be copied. All following of Christ, as we saw in a former discourse, is to have as its distinctive feature, cross-bearing; and cross-bearing is the imitation of the doing and suffering that were presented on Calvary.[5] This is the picture on which we must look in order that we may know what spirit we should be of, how we should treat the old self that is corrupt, that the new self that is redeemed may prosper—crucifying the one that the other may live, nailing to the cross the natural body, the body which the apostle describes as "the body of this death,"[6] and from which he longs to be delivered—resolutely nailing this to the cross, so that the spiritual body may grow and be in health. And it is certain that this is what is meant by having "fellowship with the sufferings" of Christ, and by "becoming conformed unto His death"; "if," to quote the apostle's language, "by any means I may attain unto the resurrection from the dead."[7]

Now the very opposite of this is to pamper and indulge this natural body, that is, to yield to, and humour, and encourage the inclinations and desires that have their root in the old sinful state of being. For self-indulgence is the very antipodes of the sacrifice of self—not only its contrast but its contradiction, that which is actively at war with the principle illustrated by the Cross, and consequently with the principle that should lie at the basis of every sincere Christian life. There are certain things connected with the old nature, features of the unregenerate condition, which may be brought over and harmonised with, and even made serviceable in the new life, but this is not one of them. The same fervour

[5] See above pp. 151-153. [6] Romans vii. 24. [7] Philippians iii. 10, 11.

which has led a man far astray in the way of sin may be so baptized by the Spirit as to carry him triumphantly forward in the way of righteousness; the gifts and talents which have, up to a certain point, been apt instruments in the work of the devil, may, through grace, become as apt in working the work of God; peculiarities and idiosyncrasies that have had full play in the region of alienation, may be brought into active requisition in the region of consecration; in a word, there are manifold elements in the character of the unconverted which may be made much account of, when, through faith, one has passed from death unto life, and from the service of Satan unto the service of God. But self-indulgence is not one of these, and never can be made one of these. It is a drawn sword against the great distinctive principle of the Christian faith; that principle which finds fullest manifestation in the Cross of Christ, and which is there exhibited that it may be recognised as the essential element that must subsist in the lives of all who accept the Crucified One as their Saviour.

And yet, as in the apostle's time, so in ours, there are many who go by the name of Christian who absolutely ignore this imperative of Christian life. They deny themselves nothing, they cannot point to the sacrifice of a single gratification for the sake of Christ. It never enters into their minds that they must yield up aught of that which pleases them in order to harmonise their practice with their profession. To speak of them crucifying themselves would be the sheerest mockery, for they have never suffered even the slightest pang, far less borne the Cross, in their pretended following of the Lord Jesus. Now, by whatever name they may be called, these are " enemies of the Cross of Christ." They are enemies in their minds, and they are enemies in their action. Their hearts are most absolutely antagonistic to the spirit which Christ displayed in dying for them. They hate with their whole nature the very idea of sacrifice of any kind, it is as repugnant to them as would be the plucking out of an eye, or the cutting off of a hand or foot. And our Saviour, well knowing this deep-rooted aversion to the principle of the Cross, makes use of these very figures in order to press home to the hearts of men the fact that sacrifice, even to the extent of excision, is necessary in respect of the old nature, if we would avoid being cast into " the Gehenna of fire." [8] But the minds of many rebel against this, and so, despite the solemn warning of the Master Himself, they will give up nothing; will make no sacrifice of inclination, desire, purpose, yield up no gratification or pleasure, incur no diminution of ease or comfort—in a word, abate not one jot or tittle of their self-indulgence, nor admit any claim of Christianity that interferes therewith.

Now this course of action on the part of professed Christians is fitted to cast discredit on the Cross of Christ. It really pours contempt on the head of the Crucified One, treats with contumely and derision that great spirit of self-abnegation that formed the very soul of His work, and practically exhibits it before the eyes of a world, only too glad to have such a thing held up to scorn, as a fanatical and quixotic disposition. Truly they are " the enemies of the Cross of Christ" who place self on the throne and not on the cross, for by every act of self-indulgence they virtually arraign and condemn Christ's

[8] Matthew xviii. 9.

great act of self-denial, and so, instead of commending that great act to the world, they set the world against it, and bar the way to acceptance of it as the means of salvation. And not more guilty was that crowd that surged around the Cross at Golgotha and derided its divine Victim than are those Christians, so-called, who show, by the whole trend of their action, that they despise the mind by which Christ was animated when he suffered there, that they will have none of it, and that they cherish within them that which is its most uncompromising antithesis. And is it not evident that, if in respect of the greatest act of the Redeemer's ministry, the professed followers of Christ will not yield Him the homage of imitation, then that ministry itself is thereby weakened in the influence which otherwise it would have over the minds of men, and the progress of the Cross, as the grand central verity of the gospel, is impeded, if not altogether stopped? The fact is, there is no more dangerous enemy of Christianity than this enemy within the camp, none whose opposition is more to be feared, and none who are more worthy of reprobation or against whom we have more need to warn.

But I pass on in the second place to note, and that with great brevity, another characteristic of the enemies of the Cross of Christ who are spoken of in our text, viz. :—their *obliquity*, as set forth in the words " whose glory is in their shame." It would be somewhat of a redeeming feature in the self-indulgent, and might form ground for hopefulness in respect of better things, if, realising the distinction between the disposition which they display, and that which animated their Master in His Cross-bearing, they were in some degree filled with contempt of themselves. It would be surely a feature indicating a certain apprehension of the character and spirit of their Master, if they recognised how mean and miserable and wretched their disposition is as compared with His. And, despite the weakness that continued to bind them to such a disposition, we might entertain expectation that a higher and nobler spirit would at length prevail, and that they would be delivered from the slavery of self, and go forth into the glorious freedom of sacrifice. But there is no redeeming quality of this nature in those of whom the apostle here speaks. On the contrary, they are not only very well satisfied with themselves, but they actually boast in those things that should make them hang their heads in shame. They glory in their success in ministering to their own gratifications. When you hear their voices exulting, it is not because, through self-denial, they have been enabled to do a Christ-like act for a fellow man, not because, by giving up some whim or gratification of their own, they have been the means of bringing some joy into the dreary life of a neighbour, nor yet because, trusting in the strength of Christ, they have triumphed over some evil passion stirring within them, and subjecting them to the bondage of sin and death. Far from any of these things are the grounds on which they congratulate themselves and glory before their fellow men. It is on account of some successful act of self-aggrandisement, because they have amassed a fortune, or outdistanced a competitor in the race for fame, or gained some one or other of the world's prizes that confer personal distinction, or in some way or other achieved a victory, of which the profits accrue to themselves alone. Now, if the spirit which animated our Lord be a right spirit, we should be ashamed of anything and everything in the benefits and blessings of which those around us cannot share. And it is simply moral obliquity to be otherwise affected. For the glorying which arises from a consideration of our own individual gratification has, as its basis, the deification of self; is, in short, self-worship, and cuts at the root of all obligation, social and religious. What spirit could be more inimical to that which was displayed on the Cross than this is? for what would have been more fatal to the whole scheme of redemption than the existence of such a spirit in the breast of the Son of God? If Christ had gloried only in that which brought gain to Himself in isolation from all others, we would have looked in vain for salvation from such a source. And is it not therefore again evident that they who exemplify this narrow spirit are of necessity "enemies of the Cross of Christ?" The fact is, that if they are right, the Cross is foolishness, and Christ Himself the greatest of all fools. You shrink, no doubt, from the very expression of this—it sounds so blasphemous—but it is the grave charge which every one, who is under the influence of the moral obliquity of which the apostle here speaks, makes against the Saviour of the world. If you are right in glorying in that which exalts and aggrandises yourself, and yourself alone, right in glorying in that which is pure and undiluted selfishness, then Christ is wrong, and foolishly wrong, for there cannot be two things right that stand so absolutely opposed to and contradictory of each other. There are not two moral standards in the universe, but only one; and since the Cross affords the supreme illustration of that one standard, they are assuredly the enemies thereof, who, by their disposition and action, would set up and glory in another. If you make a boast of that of which you should be ashamed, of your self-indulgence, your self-exaltation, your self-assertion, you are a foe of Christ Crucified, a derider of His Cross, and a partner with those who were so far left to themselves as to describe Him as mad.

But once more, another characteristic of those who are enemies of the Cross of Christ is *worldliness:* " who mind earthly things." If we go to Calvary, and realise the transaction which took place there, one thing will be made very prominent to our minds, viz., the worthlessness of all that is earthly compared with that which is spiritual. For if the Cross is fitted to do anything, it is fitted to impress upon the soul the fact that there is something far more worth the living and the dying for than aught that this world holds. The voice of the divine Sufferer said, "I, if I be lifted up from the earth, will draw all men unto Me," [9] and surely there must be an emphasis put upon the words "from the earth." To be drawn up to Christ is to be drawn up from the earth, it is to be brought into the region in which we recognise that it is a poor exchange we make if we gain the whole world and lose our own souls. And so the whole trend of the action of those who profess to be saved by Christ should be not toward but away from the world, they should not be minding earthly but heavenly things, not absorbed by material but by spiritual concerns. Now an enemy is one who sets himself to thwart and subvert that to which he is opposed. But is this not precisely what is being done in reference to the Cross of Christ by every one who is wholly taken up with earthly things? Such a one is denying, first of all, the importance

[9] John xii. 32.

of that for which Christ died—the importance of the soul and its concerns as compared with the body, the importance of eternity as compared with time, the importance of the spiritual as compared with the material. This is surely to exhibit the most pronounced enmity to the Cross, in that it is to contradict and to belittle the whole purpose for which it was reared. It is to act as if that purpose were the merest chimæra—a figment and not a reality—or, if a reality, one of far less moment than the temporal aims which the worldling sets before him.

But yet again the mind, filled with or absorbed in earthly things, is inimical to the Cross of Christ in that it sets itself against all the legitimate influences of that Cross on heart and life. It fosters those other features which we have already considered and shown to be utterly out of harmony with the spirit of Christ. All selfishness, all glorying in shame spring from it, and consequently it rears itself up against every Christ-like idea of sacrifice for the sake of our fellow-men, and shuts the heart to the entrance of those feelings which the Cross of Christ is fitted to inspire in those who yield themselves to it. Very striking is the lament of a French unbeliever who, in reference to the legend of St Francis of Assisi and the swallows, thus writes: " I am broken-hearted because of my own scepticism. The sacred stigmata will not appear in our hearts, which are dried up with selfishness; on our hands which are closed and tightened to hold fast a little gold; on our feet which are so slow to hasten to works of mercy. We are no longer able by tender speech to soothe the hungry wolf of misery, and in our low and sullen sky we can no longer summon, as with the voice of inspiration, the winged tribes which hover and sing, the divine birds of the ideal. Where are they, those fiery souls? Where are they, those scatterers of goodness like St Francis? How sweet would be a spring of hearts, a renewal of brotherhood among men. With my hand over my eyes, I question the dark horizon, but I do not see you coming, swallows, my sisters, swallows of hope and love." [10] And we *shall* question the dark horizon ever in vain so long as the spirit of the Cross is opposed by and meets with the spirit of worldliness even in those who profess to be followers of the Lord Jesus Christ. Why is it that the Cross has not more widely triumphed over the earth? Why is it not more victorious even in lands that bear the Christian name? Why are there so many, like this French sceptic, looking askance at it, and seeing in the horizon no messengers of hope and love that wing their way to the hearts of men from Calvary? Simply because there are so many professed Christians who are really the enemies of the Cross of Christ—so many who are steeped to the lips in self-indulgence instead of exhibiting the spirit of the Master—so many who glory in their shame, and that after a fashion that embitters those they should seek to win, and drives from Christ those whom they should endeavour to draw to Him—and so many who mind earthly things, thus acting in the eyes of unbelief as if this world were all, and there were no heaven to seek and no hell to dread. And until these enemies of the Cross of Christ, who have the audacity to profess the Christian name, either stand clear of the faith they dishonour, or are changed from enemies into friends, there will continue to exist an obstacle to the progress

[10] Quoted in the *British Weekly*.

of the Cross which will do it infinite harm. Let no one think he can commend the scene on Calvary by the exhibition of a spirit and of action which absolutely contravene what our Lord displayed when He suffered there. The self-indulgent, the morally oblique, and the worldly, are in the present day the greatest of barriers to the triumph of the Cross of Christ.

But in spite of all, the Cross of Christ *shall* triumph. And here there must be spoken one word to its enemies. It seeks to triumph over all such by driving forth the spirit opposed to it, and implanting the self-sacrificing spirit of the Crucified One. But if it does not accomplish this in the case of any of you, it shall triumph over you in another fashion, viz., by gaining the victory as it did over Julian the apostate —casting you down and slaying you. Rest assured, sooner or later, all Christ's enemies shall lick the dust of His feet. The prophecy shall be fulfilled, "His enemies will I clothe with shame, but upon Himself shall His crown flourish." [11] You may be certain of this that if you now glory in your shame you shall ultimately be ashamed of your glory. For if the Cross of Christ does not triumph *in* you it shall triumph *over* you. Be wise therefore, and cast down every hostile inclination and every hostile thought. Let the spirit of Christ dwell within you, let the same mind be in you which was in Christ Jesus your Lord. [12] And shrink not from those self-sacrifices to which this spirit would carry you. Christ is worthy of them all; worthy of them, because no offering you can render can ever approach in value to, far less equal that which

[11] Psalm cxxxii. 18.
[12] Phil. ii. 5.

He has rendered for you, worthy of them, because the utmost gift which, in self-denial, you can place at His feet must prove but an inadequate expression of the gratitude you owe Him, and worthy of them, because the very best and the highest of all that you can devote is only a meagre tribute to bring to the footstool of One so exalted and glorious as is the now triumphant Redeemer. For has He not right to say and plead with every one of you to-day?

> " I suffered much for thee,
>   More than thy tongue may tell,
> Of bitterest agony,
>   To rescue thee from hell.
> I suffered much for thee ;
>   What canst thou bear for Me ?
>
> And I have brought to thee,
>   Down from My home above,
> Salvation full and free,
>   My pardon and My love.
> Great gifts I brought to thee ;
>   What hast thou brought to Me ?
>
> Oh, let thy life be given,
>   Thy years for Me be spent,
> World-fetters all be riven,
>   And joy with suffering blent ;
> I gave Myself for thee :
>   Give thou thyself to Me ! " [13]

[13] Francis Ridley Havergal.

X.
PERSECUTION FOR THE CROSS.

Let us suffer with those that suffer, and be crucified with those that are crucified, that we may be glorified with those that are glorified.—MACARIUS OF ALEXANDRIA.

Ho! ye who in the noble work
   Win scorn, as flames draw air,
And in the way where lions lurk
   God's image bravely bear;
Ho! trouble-tried and torture-torn,
The kingliest kings are crowned with thorn.

. . . .

The martyr's fire-crown on the brow
   Doth into glory burn;
And tears that from love's torn heart flow
   To pearls of spirit turn.
Our dearest hopes in pangs are born,
The kingliest kings are crowned with thorn.
                    —GERALD MASSEY.

THE CROSS OF CHRIST.

X.—*PERSECUTION FOR THE CROSS.*

Galatians VI. 12.—"**Suffer persecution for the Cross of Christ.**"

The connection in which these words stand indicates clearly the sense in which they were first employed. As you may remember, when we had occasion to consider the phrase "The offence of the Cross," which occurs in the preceding chapter of the epistle to the Galatians, incidental reference had to be made to the fact that, on account of his proclamation of the Cross as the sole means of redemption, the apostle Paul had had to endure much persecution at the hands of his fellow countrymen. And it is undoubtedly to the same species of molestation that he here alludes, when in the sentence, part of which is before us, he represents his Jewish opponents as insisting on the rite of circumcision being observed, so that by their preaching of the gospel they might not incur the maltreatment to which he had been subjected. They took what they deemed a safe course, when, in proclaiming the Cross, they avoided "the offence of the Cross" by placing this old Judaic requirement alongside of it as if it were of equal moment in the matter of salvation. None of their fellow-countrymen would venture to annoy them, seeing that they did homage to the prejudices to which these so tenaciously adhered. And, as it has been somewhat quaintly put, "It was not so much out of a regard to the law as to themselves; they were willing to sleep in a whole skin and to save their worldly cargo, and cared not though they made shipwreck of faith and a good conscience. That which they chiefly aimed at was to please the Jews, and to keep up their reputation among them, and so to prevent the trouble that Paul and other faithful professors of the doctrine of Christ lay open to." [1]

It is not, however, to the conduct of these unfaithful trimmers, who to save themselves from trial tampered with truth, that I wish to draw your attention to-day, but to the experience of evil which they thereby sought to avoid, and to whatever may in these later times of the gospel correspond to that experience. And in addition to this there is a point of view, from which, for practical purposes, we may profitably regard the topic presented in our text, viz., that supplied by our Saviour Himself when, in His sermon on the Mount, He contemplated the enduring of such experiences by those who belong to His kingdom. [2] The course of our considerations may therefore be indicated as follows:

> 1st. Persecution for the Cross of Christ and its causes: (i.) as it first appeared, (ii.) as it afterwards developed in the history of the church, (iii.) as it in the present day exists;
>
> 2nd. Persecution for the Cross of Christ as a Beatitude of Christian life.

In the first place then, let us turn our attention to **Persecution for the Cross of Christ and its causes.**

---

[1] Matthew Henry, *Exposition of the Epistle to the Galatians*, on this verse.
[2] See Mat. v. 10-12.

PERSECUTION FOR THE CROSS. 177

At the outset we have to consider *this persecution and its causes as it first appeared.* I have already indicated in a former discourse the grounds on which, by reason of the Cross of Christ, those who believed in it as the sole means of salvation, and those who proclaimed it as such, rendered themselves obnoxious to the Jews, and so became victims of the malignity and the active hostility of that narrow-minded and bigoted people. It is a significant commentary on our text, and an illustration of the persecution of which it speaks, that when the apostle Paul stood in Jerusalem making his defence before his fellow-countrymen, they listened to him until he told them how his divine Master had said to him "I will send thee forth far hence unto the Gentiles," and that so soon as they heard that word, they "lifted up their voice and said, Away with such a fellow from the earth : for it is not fit that he should live."[3] And the well-understood ground of this fury of opposition was that Paul declared to those Gentiles redemption through the Cross alone—redemption apart from the law—redemption without circumcision, or any other of the ceremonial requirements of the Mosaic dispensation. It seemed monstrous to these fanatics that a salvation should be accorded to the nations beyond, which made no demand upon them for observance of rites that were esteemed so highly by the Jewish nation, and that seemed to those adhering to them to be the only method of making man acceptable to God. Very virulent was the spirit of persecution that sprung from this ; its character and measure may be judged from the cry "Away with such a fellow from the earth: for it is not fit that he should live." There was no bound

[3] Acts xxii. 21,22.

short of annihilation that would satisfy the frenzy of these zealots. It was war to the death with them against all who dared thus to cast discredit, (as they in their narrowness conceived it to be,) upon their ancient faith, and to question their pre-eminence, as the chosen people, in the sight of God. They felt, no doubt, as if they were defending their sacred patrimony, and they were consequently filled with all the utterly unreasonable hatred which is wont to be entertained against opponents by those whose vested interests and exclusive privileges are assailed. They could recognise no equality between man and man which made a like treatment of the whole human race a righteous thing on the part of God; for there lay at the root of their persecuting spirit that which has ever been most prolific of hatred and malice, viz., the mean jealousy that is not satisfied with the possession of advantages, but is full of chagrin and envy if others should come to share in similar blessings. It was not that they had the less, but that the Gentiles had the more, that quickened their malevolence; and there can be no bitterer feeling of enmity, and no more cankerous source of persecution than that which springs from this foul cause. It was the full force of this that those had to endure who first suffered "persecution for the Cross of Christ." They were regarded and treated as sacrilegious persons, who sought the ruin of the covenant; what has been called the *odium theologicum*—the keenest of religious animosities—burned fiercely against them; and there was no weapon which malice could forge, and fanaticism use, that was not employed in order to harass and molest them, and to work them woe. The most of the persecution of which we have record in the New Testament was persecution of this nature and persecution from this source. For it was not till a somewhat later period than that to which the writings of the New Testament belong, that Pagan and Roman opposition were roused and did their deadly work. In so far as it appeared in apostolic times, it was chiefly set in motion by Jewish influence, for wherever the gospel was preached, and especially wherever the Cross was held up as the only means of salvation, the Jews were wont to stir against it the passions of those amongst whom they dwelt, so that, with perhaps the exception of the uproar at Ephesus —which indeed sprang from a merely local cause—and one or two other like outbreaks, almost the entire harm which the preachers of the truth suffered, arose from the influence of which I have spoken.[4] And just on that account it was the more bitter, though it might be less effective than subsequent Gentile persecution. The apostle Paul speaks of it in terms which show how virulent and injurious it was: "Even unto this present hour we both hunger, and thirst, and are naked, and are buffeted, and have no certain dwelling-place; . . being reviled, we bless; being persecuted, we endure; being defamed, we intreat : we are made as the filth of the world, the offscouring of all things, even until now."[5]

But we must now turn to the consideration of *this persecution and its causes as it afterwards developed in the history of the Church*. For the suffering of "persecution for the Cross" of Christ was destined to assume, if not a deeper shade of malignity, in respect of its source, at least wider proportions, in respect of those who were made liable to it.

---

[4] See Acts xiii. 45 ; xiv. 2, 19 ; xvii. 5, 13 ; xviii. 12, 13, &c.
[5] 1 Cor. iv. 11-13.

And it was fraught with much more disastrous consequences than hitherto. The time, by and by arrived when the old superstitions of Paganism became alarmed at their declining supremacy, and Rome itself was roused to opposition, by fear of an influence of the Cross that seemed likely to undermine its hold upon the world. The different forms of heathenism had dwelt in peace together, and the Empire, that swayed so much of the world, was wont to tolerate all of them, and to throw the shield of protection over them, just because there was little or no antagonism between them. Errors make little attempt to uproot each other, but rather grow placidly side by side. When however the Cross was reared it could tolerate nothing that pretended to compete with it as a means of salvation, or as a way of return to God. It was and is the very essence of Christianity that it is the sole system of redemption, and its avowed aim is to subvert and bring to nought every other scheme that professes to lead to this end. It cannot tolerate these since they are false, and so tend to foil the very purpose for which the Cross was reared on Calvary. But just because of this intolerance of error, Rome, which was bound up in error, became intolerant of it. Had Christians been content to represent their faith as just one of many forms of redemption, they would never have had the experience of persecution—at least never such an experience as fell to their lot. But because the preachers of the Cross could not do this, because they were bound to declare there is only one name given under heaven amongst men by which salvation can be brought to our humanity, [6] therefore they had to endure all the evils that for centuries came upon

[6] Acts iv. 12.

them, and that, but for the sustaining hand of the great Head of the Church, would have utterly exterminated them from the face of the earth.

There is no need that I should dwell on the nature of the sufferings which they had to bear. For it is, rather the fact and the cause of that fact with which we are at present concerned. And what I wish especially to point out is, that once more it was the claim made for the Cross *as the sole means of salvation* that led to the persecution of those who clung to it. Because they elevated the Crucified Redeemer to an eminence that was entirely unique, and would have no compromise as between Him and other professed saviours of men, or as between His work and other proffered schemes of salvation, therefore they encountered the hostility and the consequent molestation of all who would not bend the knee to His name or confess that He was Lord. And thus for His name's sake they were assailed and stricken down; fellowship with Him in His sufferings became their portion; and the verity of His prediction was, through their sad experience, abundantly proved " If they have persecuted Me, they will also persecute you." [7]

When two such notable experiences of persecution for the Cross of Christ present themselves as virtually springing from the same cause, we are led to ask if this be not at all times the ground on which, by reason of acceptance of Christ Crucified, His disciples are exposed to this species of peril and evil. And I think that if we examine the testimony of history in much later times than those to which we have been referring, and even if we consider what the cause may be in

[7] John xv. 20.

the present day of anything corresponding to persecution which the Christian is called upon to suffer, we shall find that the principle which we have already observed holds true of all. It is ever the elevation of the Cross as the sole and single means of salvation that awakens the persecuting spirit. The ground on which men have suffered in all ages for their adherence to Christ and Him Crucified is precisely the ground that led to their suffering at the hands of fanatical Jews and of superstitious Pagans. At every time when there has been a recrudescence of martyrdoms, when the fires of persecution have been rekindled, and the sword of the oppressors of the faithful has been drawn, the cause is inevitably to be found in the fact that those who have been called upon to endure are such as have refused any admixture of the simple Gospel, and have clung persistently to Christ and His Cross as the only means of redemption. Was it not because they declined to admit the partnership of aught that was of human invention—of church, or priestcraft, or ritual, or saints, or virgin, or shrines, or good-works, or anything else not sanctioned by the divine word, but devised of man and begotten of tradition and myth,—I say, was it not because they declined to admit the partnership of aught of these with Christ and His Cross in the great matter of salvation that the noble army of martyrs at the era of the Reformation were constrained to lay down their lives? Did they not seal with their blood their faith in Him as the *only Saviour*—the Saviour without a rival amongst men or things? There cannot be a doubt of the fact that it was not only the pre-eminence of Christ, but *the exclusive absoluteness of Christ* as the Redeemer, and *the exclusive efficiency of His Cross* as the means of redemption for which the Reformers contended, and for which so many of them laid down their lives.

But, lastly, here, let us turn our attention to *this persecution and its causes as it in the present day exists.* If what I have said above be true, it seems to be evident that those who suffer persecution for the Cross of Christ have almost universally been those who have stood up for the honour and glory of their Redeemer. They have incurred reproach, and spoliation, and injury, in many cases even unto death, because they would not allow anything to tarnish His lustre or to dim His crown. And it seems to me that, in so far as there exists in the present day any relic of the persecuting spirit, it is chiefly directed against those who are thus jealous of the repute of their Saviour. It is a singular fact that the form of Christianity which meets with most hostility in the world is that which most exalts the Cross. Of course, in these times we are so hedged in and protected by civil enactment that the grosser aspects of persecution cannot prevail, save in lands that are practically outwith the pale of civilization, but that does not preclude those more refined manifestations that consist in imputations of hypocrisy against evangelical Christians, sneers at their scruples which prevent them from running into the same excess of riot as the world in so many instances delights in, hatred of their efforts to elevate society and to root out rampant evils, accusations of narrowness because they stand against developments and tendencies that work mischief in the midst of men and lead to ruin the unwary, and other forms of antagonism that show that the enemies are still as bitter against the Crucified One as ever in the past, and that what they lack is, not the will, but the power to sweep His disciples from the face of the earth. No, there is, in one sense, no persecution in these times, thanks to the Christianity of the past, which has reared bulwarks which the impiety of the present cannot break down, but there is latent hatred enough; and if one ventures, in the name of the Master, to try to stem some of the evil, for the removal of which from the world Christ has died, he will speedily find that, in at least a modified sense, it is possible even yet to suffer something like persecution for the Cross of Christ. And especially if he elevate that Cross into solitary prominence, and insist upon its influence as *the* paramount influence, for individual life, for the well-being of society, for the true upbuilding and regulation of the whole sphere of human affairs—that is, if he demand that the Crucified One shall be honoured and glorified in everything, it will be his to experience whatever of molestation and injury is possible in these later days. In short, one may still suffer persecution for the Cross of Christ in a thousand subtle ways, which it is true are unlike the grosser forms of the past—but only unlike them as the essence is unlike the substance, or as the spirit is unlike the body, that is, the will without the power, the force without the instrument. In this way disciples of Christ are persecuted, it may be in the home by unbelieving relations, in the workshop by ungodly co-workers, in society by sneering and sceptical associates whom they cannot avoid, and generally, in the world by those who secretly detest the Cross and all it involves. And yet they may be persecuted so subtly that it is almost impossible to describe the manner of it, or to place the finger on the word or act by which it is done. But it is there all the same, for, as I had occasion to remark in a former discourse, every genuine Christian must expect to bear the reproach of Christ, [8] and he *shall* bear that reproach precisely in proportion as he is faithful to the Cross, and as he exhibits the fulness of his trust in Him Who was crucified thereon.

We must now, however, in the second place, turn to an entirely different phase of the theme before us, viz., **Persecution for the Cross of Christ as a Beatitude of Christian life.** For this subject of persecution is one which we cannot pass from without taking into account what our Saviour Himself said regarding those who might be called upon to endure such experience. It is indeed a remarkable thing that it actually forms one of the beatitudes: "Blessed are they," said our Lord, "that have been persecuted for righteousness' sake: for theirs is the kingdom of heaven. Blessed are ye when men shall reproach you, and persecute you, and say all manner of evil against you falsely, for My sake. Rejoice, and be exceeding glad: for great is your reward in heaven: for so persecuted they the prophets which were before you." [9] It is then, in so far as we have regard to its ultimate issue, no evil at all to be persecuted for the Cross of Christ. On the contrary it is matter of congratulation to have such experience. For an experience of this nature *furnishes a seal, or attestation, or guarantee of our association with Christ and Him Crucified.* This already we might conclude from the fact that it indicates faithfulness to Christ and His Cross. No one will ever be persecuted for Him, or it, who is not closely identified with both. We cannot be persecuted for the Cross unless we are found at the

---

[8] See above pp. 151, 152.   [9] Mat. v. 10-12.

Cross, we cannot endure for Christ's sake unless we are united to Him.

But yet again, the beatitude of persecution surely also consists in the fact that *we are thereby brought into closest companionship or communion with the great Sufferer.* And is not this something to rejoice in? Who, of all the disciples of our Lord, would not rather suffer with Paul than reign with Nero, be imprisoned with Peter than feast with Herod, be martyred with Stephen than pass judgment with Caiaphas? Would not every genuine Christian esteem it of moment to have co-experience with those who have sealed their faithfulness by their sufferings? Would it not be an honour to stand side by side with them? But through persecution for the Cross of Christ we come into even a higher and better fellowship. For, when we look back upon the long line of martyrs who have yielded themselves up to death for the sake of the truth, does not His name occupy the supremely highest place "Who endured the Cross despising the shame?" [10] And every one enters into close association with Him who suffers for His name's sake. Surely to be thus identified, and brought into most intimate communion and holiest brotherhood with Christ, involves the highest and most perfect blessedness, a blessedness for the attainment of which all crosses, and perils, and enmities may be accounted as nothing, and may with ease and even with rejoicing be borne.

But, still further, I remark that, to suffer persecution for the Cross of Christ may be esteemed a beatitude in that *it is accompanied by the consciousness of suffering in a good cause.* To sacrifice one's ease, or well-being, or life, for some high

[10] Heb. xii. 2.

and holy principle brings no small measure of satisfaction and happiness to the sincere and honest heart. How great, therefore, must be, and is the joy of the faithful disciples who realise that, whatever of persecution they endure, is due to their fealty to the Master, and that, instead of bringing disgrace upon them, it is fitted to reflect honour on their characters and to shed lustre on their names.

Then again, I remark that the persecuted for the Cross of Christ are blessed in that *their sufferings become the best means of their spiritual advancement.* That which the world would fain quell by its opposition and enmity is only made the stronger thereby. The souls and lives of Christians are purified by tribulation as gold is refined in the fire. They are burned clear of those spots, and that dimness which reveal the presence of an alloy. Persecution thus becomes the true pathway of progress for the Church and for the disciple; and such the apostle recognised it to be, when, longing for that perfection to which he had not yet attained, he expressed his desire to reach it through "fellowship of the sufferings" of Christ and by "being made comformable unto His death."[11] In an eminent degree do persecutions work together for good to those that love God.[12] For has not the church by means of them been extended and strengthened, built up and clarified? Is not "the blood of the martyrs the seed of the church"?[13] And shall not the trials of persecution serve an analogous purpose in individual life?

But once more, and finally, to suffer persecution for the

---

[11] Phil. iii. 10.

[12] Being pre-eminently distinguished amongst the "all things" to which the apostle refers as securing this end, Rom. viii. 28.

[13] *Semen est sanguis Christianorum,* Tertullian, *Apol.* cap. 50.

Cross of Christ is to enter into beatitude in that *it is to enter into the prospect of eternal reward.* And this prospect itself, even ere the attainment of that reward, may bring rejoicing. We may indeed " count it all joy " to suffer if thereby we come at last to reign. The promise of Christ is very explicit, " theirs is the kingdom of heaven." Even in the midst of all molestation or disadvantage on earth, this kingdom may fill the eyes of the disciple, and absorb his thought—this kingdom, with its white robes, and palms, and crowns, and thrones;—this kingdom, with its transcendent beauty, and eternal felicity;—this kingdom, in which they who have "come out of great tribulation, and have washed their robes, and made them white in the blood of the Lamb," are ever " before the throne of God ; and serve Him day and night in His temple." [14] And to join this blessed multitude, to mingle with "the noble army of Martyrs," to unite in "the goodly fellowship of the Prophets," to stand in "the glorious company of the Apostles," to come unto "the general assembly and church of the first-born who are enrolled in heaven, and to God the Judge of all, and to the spirits of just men made perfect, and to Jesus the Mediator of a new Covenant," to enter into "the city of the living God, the heavenly Jerusalem," and to associate with " the innumerable hosts of angels," [15] and to enjoy all the blessedness which such high and holy communion implies throughout the ages of eternity—is not this a prospect which may so raise one, out of the suffering of persecution into the joy of it, as to constrain the acknowledgment that "our light affliction, which is but for the moment, worketh for us more and more exceedingly an eternal weight

[14] Rev. vii. 9-17. [15] *Te Deum* and Heb. xii. 22-24.

of glory," [16] and that "the sufferings of this present time are not worthy to be compared with the glory which shall be revealed to us-ward"? [17] So far from adopting, as did the Jews referred to in the words that precede our text, any unworthy means, in order to escape the suffering of persecution for the Cross of Christ, the disciple has rather reason to welcome such, should it come in a legitimate way, and like the apostles, to rejoice that he is counted "worthy to suffer dishonour for the Name" of Jesus. [18] For, as we shall have occasion to emphasise in next discourse, when we proceed to consider the last of these passages on the Cross of Christ, this is a shame in which we may well glory, a shadow in time which brings lustre in eternity, a dishonour amongst men which leads on to highest distinction before God.

Let us then be ready, at any and every time, should we be called upon to do so, to suffer persecution for the Cross of Christ. We cannot endure in a higher, a nobler, or a more worthy cause. It is even now a distinction to be marked for obloquy on account of the fidelity we show to the Crucified Christ. And it is the blessing of blessings as well. For what the poet has sung in respect of all cross-bearing we may sing in respect of this particular form of it:

"Heavier the cross, the nearer heaven;
  No cross without, no God within!
Death, judgment from the heart are driven,
  Amid the world's false glare and din.
    Oh, happy he, with all his loss,
    Whom God hath set beneath the cross.

"Heavier the cross, the better Christian;
  This is the touchstone God applies.
How many a garden would be wasting
  Unwet by showers from weeping eyes!

[16] 2 Cor. iv. 17. [17] Rom. viii. 18. [18] Acts v. 41.

THE CROSS OF CHRIST.

The gold by fire is purified ;
The Christian is by trouble tried.

" Heavier the cross, the stronger faith :
  The loaded palm strikes deeper root ;
The vine-juice sweetly issueth
  When men have pressed the clustered fruit ;
    And courage grows where dangers come,
    Like pearls beneath the salt sea-foam.

" Heavier the cross, the heartier prayer ;
  The bruised herbs most fragrant are.
If sky and wind were always fair
  The sailor would not watch the star ;
    And David's Psalms had ne'er been sung
    If grief his heart had never wrung.

" Heavier the cross, the more aspiring ;
  From vales we climb to mountain-crest ;
The pilgrim, of the desert tiring,
  Longs for the Canaan of his rest.
    The dove has here no rest in sight,
    And to the ark she wings her flight.

" Heavier the cross, the easier dying ;
  Death is a friendlier face to see ;
To life's decay one bids defying,
  From life's distress one then is free.
    The cross sublimely lifts our faith
    To Him Who triumphed over death.

" Thou Crucified ! the cross I carry,
  The longer, may it dearer be ;
And lest I faint while here I tarry,
  Implant Thou such a heart in me
    That faith, hope, love may flourish there,
    Till for the cross my crown I wear." [19]

[19] Benjamin Schmolk.

XI.
GLORYING IN THE CROSS.

Lamb, the once crucified! Lion, by triumph surrounded!
Victim all bloody, and Hero, Who hell hast confounded!
      Pain-riven heart,
        That from earth's deadliest smart
        O'er all the heavens hast bounded.

Thou in the depths wert to mortals the highest revealing,
God in humanity veiled, Thy full glory concealing!
      " Worthy art Thou!"
      Shouteth eternity now,
      Praise to Thee endlessly pealing.

. . . .

Join O my voice! the vast chorus, with trembling emotion:
Chorus of saints, who, though sundered by land and by ocean,
      With sweet accord
      Praise the same glorious Lord,
      One in their ceaseless devotion.

Break forth O nature! in song, when the spring-tide is nighest!
World that hast seen His salvation, no longer thou sighest!
      Shout, starry train,
      From your empyreal plain,
      " Glory to God in the highest!"

                          —META HEUSSER SCHWEIZER

THE CROSS OF CHRIST.

XI.—GLORYING IN THE CROSS.

Galatians VI. 14.—"God forbid that I should glory, save in the Cross of our Lord Jesus Christ."

To-day we are brought to the consideration of the final topic presented to us by the passages in the New Testament in which specific mention is made of the Cross of Christ. The course we have already pursued has led us into the contemplation of many of the most rich and varied truths that connect themselves with the sufferings of our Lord; for, whilst we have lingered Sabbath after Sabbath at Calvary, the great transaction there has assumed manifold aspects, its essential meaning has, I trust, been more clearly revealed to us, and its far reaching effects have been more completely apprehended. We have had opportunity of seeking to realise the spirit of absolute self-surrender in which our Saviour gave Himself to be the Sacrifice for sin, how He became "obedient even unto death, yea, the death of the Cross," how He "endured the Cross, despising the shame"; we have had occasion to enquire into the gracious purpose which He had in view in laying down His life, the making of "peace through the blood of His Cross," the reconciling of man "unto God in one body by the Cross," and the taking away of the commandment of ordinances, "nailing it to His Cross"; we have been called upon to consider the twofold effect of the Cross,

to one the savour of life unto life, to the other of death unto death, in that the preaching of the Cross is "to them that are perishing foolishness; but to us which are being saved the power of God"; we have also had before our minds the obstacles to the legitimate effects of Christ's sufferings, obstacles which constitute "the offence of the Cross," and which raise up "enemies of the Cross of Christ"; and last Sabbath our thoughts were fixed upon the beatitude of endurance into which the disciple who comes in faith to the Crucified One may be called upon to enter, in that it may be his lot to "suffer persecution for the Cross of Christ."[1] And now today we come to a theme which, as it seems to me, forms a fitting sequel to all that has gone before, and a fitting conclusion to the sacred study in which we have been engaged. For, if we have apprehended rightly the truths which are set forth in the passages which have been already considered, and if we have received with any degree of fulness these verities into our minds and hearts, then it is very certain that the spirit induced in us should be such as will only find adequate expression in the words of our text: "God forbid that I should glory save in the Cross of our Lord Jesus Christ."

I have already, in former discourses, explained the reason why the apostle Paul exhibits the Cross so prominently, and exalts it so highly in this epistle to the Galatians. It was to counteract the evil influence of certain teachers who, afraid of the offence of it, sought to belittle it, and to hold up the old ceremonialism of the Jewish law as of equal account. As against the pernicious doctrines which these tried to

[1] For the various passages see p. 15.

disseminate, the apostle emphasised Christ Crucified as the sole means of salvation ; he would not, in the face of their aberration, abate one jot or tittle of the claim he made for the Cross to be, not merely the pre-eminent, but the absolute and exclusive ground of redemption. These erroneous teachers had however been successful in leading not a few astray from the simplicity of the gospel, and this appears to have induced in them a vain-glorious spirit. They boasted of the number of their proselytes, of the righteousness which these and themselves exhibited in obeying the law, and of the fair shew which they consequently made in the flesh. [2] Now to this glorying Paul opposes himself with all the earnestness of his nature. If in such things there was cause for boasting then might he with more reason than those of whom he wrote lift up his voice in pride. He was formerly a Pharisee, "touching the righteousness which is in the law, blameless." But what things were gain to him those he counted loss for Christ. [3] And although, subsequent to his conversion, he had been singularly honoured in being the instrument by which very many had been brought to the truth, yet of these he would make no boast. He would only glory in that which the vanity of those whom he rebuked cast into the shade ;— the salvation wrought out by the suffering of his Lord, from which proceeded both his own righteousness and the righteousness of all those who through him were led within the influence of the faith : " God forbid that I should glory save in the Cross of our Lord Jesus Christ."

In so far as his own experience was concerned, it is probable that Paul found a cause—not by any means the whole

[2] Gal. vi. 12.   [3] See Phil. iii. 4-9.

cause—but a cause for his glorying in the Cross in the fact which, in the words succeeding our text he records. For the Cross was that "through which"[4] as he avers "the world hath been crucified unto me, and I unto the world." There had flowed from it a sacred influence which had entirely severed Paul from the world, and which made him look upon it and all its concerns as withered and dead, in comparison with the great things pertaining to the Cross. The world was crucified unto him. All its glory had passed away from his eyes. He beheld in it no longer any supreme attraction on which to set his heart or of which to make his boast. He had had his eyes opened to behold glories in comparison with which all the earthly and transitory are mere glitter and tinsel. And hence also he in turn was crucified unto the world. To use his own graphic language, he was "dead with Christ,"[5] dead as to his old nature, his old affections and lusts. The vain show that moved before him from day to day no more affected him than it could affect those who had passed away from this mortal scene. He lived in another sphere, for all his thoughts, hopes, and aspirations centred in and clustered round the Cross of his Lord. And in another sense as well were he and the worldly sundered from each other through the Cross of Christ, for as Luther has expressed it, he may be regarded as virtually saying, "The world is crucified to me, *i.e.*, I account that the world is condemned; and even so

---

[4] "*Through which*," according to the more exact translation of the Revised Version; not "*by whom*" as in the Authorised Version. In either case, however, the meaning is practically the same, for whilst "through which" refers directly to the Cross—the main theme of the passage—"by whom" must of necessity refer to Christ Crucified.

[5] Rom. vi. 8.

am I in turn crucified unto the world, *i.e.*, it accounts that I am condemned. Thus we condemn one another. I anathematize all its human righteousness, doctrine, and work, as the very devil's poison, and it in return anathematizes also my doctrine and work, and counts me for a mischievous man." [6] And, because of all this, Paul will glory in the Cross of Christ, in it and in nothing else. His personal experience leads him to such exaltation of it.

But even above and transcending personal experience there were and are elements connected with it which were and are fitted to make all who cling to it for salvation glory in it, and not only glory in it, but realise as well that there is nothing else so well worth the glorying in, that it is befitting to set it up in solitary pre-eminence above all things, for in comparison with its lustre all the glories of earth fade into nothingness and pass away. For this exclamation of the apostle to which our attention is turned to-day, although it arises out of particular circumstances such as I have sought to explain, and connects itself with a specific personal experience, recorded, as we have seen, in the words that follow our text, is nevertheless an exclamation appropriate to the lips of every one who is relying for salvation on the finished work of the Lord Jesus Christ. There are grounds upon which every disciple may take his stand in echoing the language of the apostle—reasons why he should declare his determination to glory in nothing else save the Cross, why he should refuse to bring into comparison or competition with it anything, however illustrious it may be,

[6] Quoted in Schmoller's *Commentary on the Epistle to the Galatians* (Lange's Edn.), p. 160.

of an earthly or human nature. For, as we contemplate the scene at Calvary, and gather its meaning both as it affects ourselves and as it affects our fellowmen, and trace out its past results and its future possibilities, there comes to us with a new meaning the Old Testament injunction, which we might almost think the apostle had before his mind when he penned our text: "Thus saith the Lord, let not the wise man glory in his wisdom, neither let the mighty man glory in his might, let not the rich man glory in his riches: but let him that glorieth glory in this, that he understandeth, and knoweth Me, that I am the Lord which exercise lovingkindness, judgment, and righteousness, in the earth: for in these things I delight, saith the Lord." [7]

Let us seek to state to ourselves some of the more prominent reasons why the disciple of Christ should above all things glory in the Cross of Christ. What has been already said indicates that these reasons are of two kinds, general and specific; reasons that connect themselves with the far-reaching verities that in the Cross find their centre, and reasons that connect themselves with the individual experiences that in the Cross have their source. Following the line of thought which this suggests, I propose in succession to note that

  1st. The believer should glory in the Cross because of the place it occupies in the world;

  2nd. The believer should glory in the Cross because of the place it occupies in his own heart and life.

First then, I remark that **the believer should glory in the Cross of Christ because of the place it**

[7] Jer. ix. 23, 24

occupies in the world. I think that it may be said that even the external aspect of that scene which presents itself to our eyes on Calvary proclaims it to be the most remarkable and significant event in the world's history, and, so far as we know, the most remarkable and significant event in the annals of the universe. And there are features in this external aspect that bring us into touch with the internal truths that are by this event both created and shadowed forth. Let us once more regard some of the particulars of it, and see whither they may lead us, and especially see if there is aught in them that should occasion glorying on our part, or on the part of any one, on account of this singular transaction. Certainly at first sight there seems little to glory in, rather much that may bring the blush of shame to the cheek, and a rush of horror to the heart. Three crosses are reared in this place, reared not far from the holy city, and within sight of the sacred temple of the one living and true God. On two of these crosses are raised criminals of the lowest and vilest type, who, according to the confession of one of them, suffer justly for the deeds which they have committed. [8] Between them, lifted up to pre-eminence as if He were the worst of all, there is nailed One, the purity and innocence of Whose life has been such that not even His most virulent enemies have been able to bring against Him any evidence of evil, One Whose whole conduct has been, by word and work, to do good and confer richest blessing on those who now crucify Him, One Who has declared Himself to be the Messiah for Whom His crucifiers profess to have long and ardently sought, and Who, by

[8] Luke xxiii. 41.

wondrous deeds and still more wondrous speech, has revealed His mission and justified His claim. And now, on Golgotha, we behold Him put to a most shameful and cruel death by the very hands of those to whom, and for whom He came, nailed to the Cross a Victim of the malice of the rulers and the fury of the populace, exposed, even in His last agonies, to bitter derision and reproach, an object of scorn and railing to the scum and offscourings of the human race.

But in marvellous contrast to the wild storm of the sea of wickedness that is raging around Him is every gesture, look, and word of the Crucified One. We hear from Him not bitterness and cursing against His enemies, but the language of meekness and blessing. Was ever such prayer as now comes from His lips uttered in such circumstances: "Father, forgive them; for they know not what they do"[9]? His sufferings cannot stem the tide of His mercy and compassion, for to one of the malefactors He speaks the word of pardon and acceptance, "To-day thou shalt be with Me in Paradise."[10] Even in the midst of His own sorrows He consigns His weeping mother to the care of a beloved disciple."[11] And then, as the shadows of death gather over His spirit, the mysterious cry breaks forth, "My God, My God, why hast Thou forsaken Me?"[12] To human weakness calling for the drink of cold water[13] there succeeds divine strength declaring "It is finished,"[14] and then there follows the language of calm and confident resignation, "Father, into Thy hands I commend My spirit."[15] And with such words of peaceful faith,

---

[9] Luke xxiii. 34.   [10] *Ibid.* v. 43.   [11] John xix. 26, 27.
[12] Mat. xxvii. 46.   [13] John xix. 28.   [14] *Ibid* v. 30.
[15] Luke xxiii. 46.

the mighty Sufferer bows His head, and gives up the ghost. What signs and portents that moment reveals! The very sun in the heavens refuses its light, the earth trembles, the rocks cleave asunder, the veil of the temple is rent in twain![16] Thus even the external aspect of this event is such as to single it out from all others, and the Pagan centurion standing by, having heard probably of the claim made by this strange Sufferer, has conviction brought home to his heart in the moment of crisis, and involuntarily exclaims, "Truly this was the Son of God!"[17]

It is this that most directly leads us from the external aspect of the scene to its inner reality, this that enables us to harmonise the strange contrast between the surroundings of the Sufferer and the character and spirit of the Sufferer Himself. That contrast is an enigma till we know that this is no other than "the Son of God," that this is no other than the Deity Himself bending unto death, laying down His life as a divine Sacrifice. In this event the prophetic predictions become history : " He was wounded for our transgressions, He was bruised for our iniquities : . . . the Lord hath laid on Him the iniquity of us all."[18] And herein we have that which changes what would otherwise be only a scene to be viewed with inextinguishable shame and horror into a scene in which we may well glory—that which has transformed the Cross so completely that, whereas it had erewhile been the very climax of disgrace, and the object of utter detestation, it has become the most lustrous emblem in the universe, and, in respect of its significance, the object of the most profound

[16] Mat. xxvii. 45, 51-53; Mark xv. 38; Luke xxiii. 44, 45.
[17] Mat. xxvii. 54.   [18] Isa. liii. 5, 6.

adoration and love. For it was not the sight of suffering innocence, not the sight of triumphant malice and cruelty, not the sight of evil apparently victorious which evoked the declaration of the apostle that is to-day before us, but something lying behind these merely eternal aspects—viz., the fact, so well apprehended by Paul, that on that Cross sin was expiated, justice satisfied, holiness vindicated, the way of salvation opened up to the human race, and, above all, such a revelation made of the yearning toward man of the divine heart, and of the plan and aim of the divine love, as had never been possible before. In all this the apostle found ground of exultation; it was this that constrained him to write, and it is this that may constrain every disciple to exclaim, "God forbid that I should glory save in the Cross of our Lord Jesus Christ."

Now taking a comprehensive view of what has just been before us, I think we may say that we have reason to glory in the Cross of Christ above all other things because it is *man's key to the nature of God.* Blot out the scene on Calvary from the records of inspiration, and what a blank is produced in the revelation of the divine character and plans. Without this event all else that God has ever made known to man becomes an enigma, a riddle which cannot be read. Without this we would hopelessly strive to pierce through the darkness which surrounds the throne of the Almighty, and, even were we successful in finding God, we should not find the Father. But the light streaming from the Cross dispels all the mist, and actually lays bare to us the very heart of the Eternal One in its paternal longings for us. "All His revelations in the Old Testament, His ordinances, institutions, promises, judgments" in the Cross "reach their fulfilment and find their real explanation." Nay more, "all the hints of truth current among heathen nations—all their sighing and striving after the knowledge of God and communion with Him, all attempts to get rid of the consciousness of guilt, to atone for sin and to effect a perfect restoration to divine favour—in short everything regarding the nature of God and His designs which glimmered as a ray of light here and there in this darkness, obtains in Christ and in Christ Crucified its goal," because in Him it finds its full manifestation. [19] In the Cross we have revealed most perfectly every one of the divine attributes. Behold, for example, the infinite *love* of God ; "Scarcely for a righteous man will one die : for peradventure for the good man some would even dare to die. But God commendeth His own love toward us, in that while we were yet sinners, Christ died for us." [20] Behold again the divine *power*. On the Cross, Christ "spoiled principalities and powers, and made a shew of them openly, triumphing over them in it," [21] on it He "brought to nought him who had the power of death, that is, the devil," [22] wresting from him his dominion over the hearts and lives of men. Behold also the *righteousness* of God ; He "spared not His own Son, but delivered Him up for us all," [23] that "He might be just, and the Justifier of him that hath faith in Jesus." [24] In short, behold in and through the Cross every feature of the divine nature—His *wisdom*, His *holiness*, His *justice*, His *truth*, His *mercy*,—every feature that belongs to His relation to us, and to His purposes on our behalf.

---

[19] See Stier, *The Words of the Lord Jesus* on Mat v. 17 in Vol. I. pp. 124-140.
[20] Rom. v. 7.   [21] Col. ii. 15.   [22] Heb. ii. 14.   [23] Rom. vii. 32.
[24] Rom. iii. 26.

There is not a spot in the whole universe from which we can obtain such a view of the attributes of God. Here they are concentrated and focussed so that the revelation of them falls upon us with tenfold power. Here are made known the riches, and the glory, and the infinitude of them. In a word, if we would realise all that God is, and all that He has done for us, and all that He is yet willing to do for us, if we would realise Him in the perfect harmony of all the features of His character, we must view Him as He makes Himself known in and through the Cross. And, because of this, surely we, and all other believers, have reason to glory in the Cross, which thus makes so signally manifest to us the divine nature, illumining our darkness, dispelling our ignorance, correcting our misconceptions, and revealing God as far more loving, far more gracious, and far more full of long-suffering than we had ever conceived Him to be. When we look upon it as the highest interpreter to man of the attitude toward, and the designs regarding him, of his heavenly Father, we wonder no longer that, despite the shame and obloquy that at one time attached to this object of suffering, it should now be fitting for every believer to exclaim, "God forbid that I should glory save in the Cross of our Lord Jesus Christ."

But once more I remark that we have reason to glory in the Cross of Christ because it is *God's lever for the restoration of man.* It is not only that it reveals the divine nature and the divine purpose, but it is that it is the great and efficient means whereby this divine purpose is carried out. On the Cross atonement is made for sin, pardon is procured for the sinner, the work of grace is carried out to its last requisite, and everything perfected that pertains to the plan of redemption.

And therefore from it, as from a fountainhead, flow forth those mighty energies which are efficient to raise fallen humanity out of the condition of degradation into which it has sunk, and to bring it to God-like eminence. And from this point of view, what a grand object the Cross of Christ becomes! Consider the countless millions of men who, from first to last, have been redeemed and sanctified by its mighty power. Consider the change it has produced on their lives here and now; the uplifting and ennobling effect it has had upon them; the transformation in their character through the supplanting of every vice by its contrasting virtue; the radical alteration in the essence of human nature of which this is the outward sign—an alteration so great that it can only be compared to that from death to life, from slavery to freedom. Consider as well the changed outlook for man that has issued from the Cross of Christ; a change effected by the fact that, through the Cross, reconciliation has been effected between him and his heavenly Father, so that his eternal destiny is no longer an everlasting alienation, but a heavenly home. Consider all the comfort, and aid, and consolation, and direction that are imparted through the gospel to man on his way thitherward. Then look to the goal itself, and consider the glory reserved in it for the great multitude "who have washed their robes, and made them white in the blood of the Lamb," [25] and who with one heart and voice ascribe "unto Him that sitteth upon the throne, and unto the Lamb, the blessing, and the honour, and the glory, and the dominion, for ever and ever." [26] Consider the whole lustre of heaven and compare it with the eternal gloom of hell, the joy

[25] Rev. vii. 14. [26] Rev. v. 13.

of the former and the misery of the latter—a joy and a misery that, we may say, lie backward on human life, the one projecting its shadow even to the cradle of the natural birth, and the other shedding its light upon the first spiritual experiences of those who are born again—consider this contrast, for it is the summation of the whole, and then declare if that which saves from the sorrow of the one, and quickens to the happiness of the other, is not an object to boast of and glory in above and beyond everything else. And the reasons for glorying in the Cross are of even fuller force now than they were in Paul's day; for not only is it the case that the light streaming from the Cross down through time has not lost its brilliance through the lapse thereof, not only is it true that it is fitted to exercise the same influence now as in his day, but there is this further, that we have in history a most glorious testimony to, and certitude of that stupendous and hallowed influence, that we have therefore that which has, year by year, and century by century, enhanced the lustre of the Cross, and made it manifest as more and more worthy of being gloried in.

But in the second place I remark that **the believer should glory in the Cross of Christ because of the place it occupies in his own heart and life.** I do not think it necessary to enter at all upon the development of this side of our subject, for the nature of the reasons for glorying in the Cross that arise from specific individual experiences, has been already sufficiently set forth in our consideration of what the apostle testifies in the words succeeding our text as to the effect of the Cross upon his life. And in view of this it will suffice to say that, in proportion as we are crucified unto the world, and the world crucified unto us, we shall feel disposed to glory in the Cross—that is, we shall glory in it in proportion as we obtain the victory through it. We shall have pride in it, as men have pride in the standard under which they fight, we shall glory in it, as the source of our inspiration, and the fountain as well of all our good. And we shall regard it as strange that men can or should glory in aught else. For what, of all the objects of human exultation, can for a moment compare with this? There are those who glory in wisdom: but whilst their wisdom shall perish that of the Cross is eternal in that it makes man "wise unto salvation";[27] there are those who glory in their power: but even the powers of the heavens shall be shaken, and how much more all earthly might,—it shall vanish as smoke and be as nothing—but the power of the Cross is among the things that cannot be shaken, and shall for ever remain;[28] there are those who glory in their fame: but the wreath of fame shall wither as the grass of the morning, whilst the names of those who are written in heaven shall be lustrous through eternity, with a lustre begotten of the confession of them by Christ before His and their heavenly Father;[29] there are those who glory in wealth: but it is dross which shall be burned up in the conflagration of worlds, and even were it to continue, what is it compared with the "inheritance incorruptible, and undefiled, and that fadeth not away"?[30] there are those who glory in pleasure: but all earthly pleasures are as pain in

[27] See 2 Tim. iii. 15, compare 1 Cor. i. 21-25, ii. 6, 7.
[28] See Heb. xii. 27, 28; 1 Pet. i. 24, 25.
[29] See Luke x. 20; Mat. x. 32; Col. iii. 4.
[30] See 2 Pet. iii. 10; 1 Pet. i. 4.

comparison with the "joy unspeakable" that is the disciple's portion;[31] and there are manifold other objects in which this world glories: but even were these all summed together—the best, the highest, the most lasting of them,—they are utterly unworthy even of a single thought when we put them in the scale over against the Cross of Christ. "God forbid that I should glory save in the Cross of our Lord Jesus Christ"— the Cross which has unveiled to me the loving heart of the heavenly Father [32]—the Cross which has revealed to me my need of the Father's heart [33]—the Cross which has brought me nigh to the experience of the Father's love [34]—the Cross which is the pledge of my acceptance by the Father's hand [35] —the Cross which fits me for the fellowship of the Father's mind [36]—the Cross which makes me triumph over all that opposes the Father's will [37]—the Cross which leads me safely on the way to the Father's house [38]—the Cross which is the key that unlocks the gate of the Father's city [39]—the Cross which brings me at length into the Father's presence [40]—the

[31] See 1 Pet. i. 8; 1 Cor. ii. 9.
[32] John iii. 16: "God so loved the world, that He gave His only begotten Son."
[33] John xvi. 7: "It is expedient for you that I go away," compare John xi. 49-52.
[34] Eph. ii. 13: "Made nigh in the blood of Christ."
[35] 2 Cor. v. 19: "God was in Christ reconciling the world unto Himself."
[36] Col. i. 22: "Reconciled ... through death, to present you holy and without blemish and unreproveable before Him."
[37] 1 John v. 5: "Who is he that overcometh the world, but he that believeth?"
John xiv. 2: "In My Father's house are many mansions; ... I go to prepare a place for you."
[39] 2 Pet. i. 11: "Thus shall be richly supplied unto you the entrance into the eternal kingdom."
[40] Jude 24: "Now unto Him that is able ... to set you before the presence of His glory."

Cross which procures for me at last the Father's gracious reward [41]—the Cross which brings to the Crown. [42]

> "In the Cross of Christ I glory,
>   Towering o'er the wrecks of time;
> All the light of sacred story
>   Gathers round its head sublime.
>
> When the woes of life o'ertake me,
>   Hopes deceive, and fears annoy,
> Never shall the Cross forsake me;
>   Lo, it glows with peace and joy.
>
> When the sun of bliss is beaming
>   Light and love upon my way,
> From the Cross the radiance streaming
>   Adds more lustre to the day.
>
> Bane and blessing, pain and pleasure,
>   By the Cross are sanctified;
> Peace is there that knows no measure,
>   Joys that through all time abide.
>
> In the Cross of Christ I glory,
>   Towering o'er the wrecks of time;
> All the light of sacred story
>   Gathers round its head sublime." [43]

[41] Mat. xxv. 34: "Come, ye blessed of My Father, inherit the kingdom."
[42] 2 Tim. iv. 8: "The crown of righteousness, which the Lord ... shall give;" Rev. ii. 10: "Be thou faithful unto death, and I will give thee a crown of life."
[43] Sir John Bowring.

By This Conquer.

THE
PREACHER'S IDEAL.

We ought to speak affectionately and devotedly, simply, candidly, and with confidence; to be filled and occupied with the doctrine we wish to teach, and with the conclusion we desire to press upon the audience. The sovereign artifice is to have no artifice; our words ought to be warmed, not by cries and exaggerated actions, but by inward affection, and to come from the heart, not merely from the lips. It has been well said, that the tongue speaks only to the ears; but the heart speaks to the heart.

—Francis de Sales.

THE PREACHER'S IDEAL.

A SERMON DELIVERED IN ERSKINE CHURCH, FALKIRK,
ON SABBATH, JANUARY 19TH, 1896.

Acts XX. 27.—"I have not shunned to declare unto you all the counsel of God."

For a period of upwards of two years the apostle Paul had preached the gospel in the city of Ephesus, "reasoning daily," as we are told "in the school of Tyrannus."[1] The result of this ministry was the founding and upbuilding of one of the most active and flourishing churches in Asia Minor. Such success indeed had attended the efforts put forth that those who were interested in the worship of the great goddess Diana took alarm, and made an endeavour, through violence, to bring to nought the good cause. In this they were notably unsuccessful, but it was deemed expedient that the apostle should leave the city, and entrust to the native leaders and teachers the carrying on of the work which he had so well begun.[2] This he did, after duly providing for the maintenance of the church by the ordaining of elders and pastors, as was his wont in every Christian community which was formed by his labours. Thereafter he had gone to Macedonia and Greece, exhorting and confirming those whom he had already led to the faith, and, as well, no doubt, laying the basis of other branches of the Church of Christ.[3] And

[1] Acts xix. 9, 10. [2] *Ibid.* v. 23. [3] Acts xx. 1, 2.

now, after a lengthened absence, he had returned to the shores of Asia Minor, for, on his way back to Jerusalem, he put in at the sea port of Miletus, which lay some thirty-six miles to the south of Ephesus.[4] This afforded him an opportunity, eagerly embraced, of renewing for a little his fellowship with those whom he had won to the gospel in the latter city. He sent for the elders of the church, and, when they were come, he delivered to them the striking and affecting address in the midst of which the words of our text occur. In that address he goes back upon the facts of his ministry amongst them, and, in the confidence of a clear conscience, declares, in language that, save for the stamp of honesty it bears, might seem to savour of egotism, how he had faithfully, and without fear of man, discharged his obligations to them and to his Master, as a preacher of the word. He can indeed make appeal to their own knowledge of how he demeaned himself whilst he was in their midst, and this was, no doubt, an important factor lying behind the address, and fitted to quicken into a special sense of responsibility those who listened to it. Whatever use they had made of his ministry, so far as he himself was concerned, he could boldly affirm, "Wherefore I testify unto you this day, that I am pure from the blood of all men. For I shrank not from declaring unto you the whole counsel of God."[5]

It is to the latter part of this statement that I desire to direct your attention to-day, for it contains the pith or marrow, of, at least, the first portion of the discourse of the apostle; is, so to speak, a summary of the record of his ministry amongst the Ephesians. And it is such a summary

[4] Acts xx. 15.   [5] As rendered in the Revised Version.

as contains suggestive elements both for preachers and for hearers—for the former, in that it sets forth the nature of the commission they bear, for the latter, in that it indicates what they have reason to expect and to require from every ambassador for Christ. It were well if, in the face of those to whom he has ministered, every pastor and teacher were able to say, after his period of service was over, " I shrank not from declaring unto you the whole counsel of God." For this is, at least, the ideal of a Christian ministry, the purpose which every faithful servant who labours in the cause of the gospel should have before him, the obligation which he should seek to discharge, as due to his Lord, and due to those over whom he is placed in the Lord. And there are one or two things about this ideal to which I think I may, to-day, profitably draw your attention, for although it may seem that our text is one that more especially suits the minister himself, yet there are views suggested by it that may be of equal value to both pastor and people.

There are three points that seem to me to demand attention, and these may be stated as follows :—

> 1st. The limits of the preacher's commission : " The *counsel* of God " ;
> 2nd. The extent of the preacher's commission : " The *whole* counsel of God " ;
> 3rd. The preacher's temptation : To "*shrink* from declaring the whole counsel of God."

First then let me call your attention to *the limits of the preacher's commission:* " The *counsel* of God." There can be no doubt that the apostle means by the phrase now before us the divine purpose and plan of redemption and all the adjuncts thereto. This involves the sacred Scriptures, leading to their climax in Christ—the divine word, from beginning to end, conducting to Him Who is Himself the Living Word. We can be under no misapprehension as to the character of the message with which every one who is set apart to speak for Christ is charged, if we but give heed to the Master's own directions when sending forth His disciples after His resurrection and before His ascension. Very significant is the passage in Luke which records the manner in which He commissioned these men to carry abroad the tidings of His Gospel to all the ends of the earth. "He said unto them, These are My words which I spake unto you, while I was yet with you, how that all things must needs be fulfilled, which are written in the law of Moses, and the prophets, and the psalms, concerning Me. Then opened He their mind, that they might understand the Scriptures; and He said unto them, Thus it is written, that the Christ should suffer, and rise again from the dead the third day; and that repentance and remission of sins should be preached in His name unto all nations, beginning from Jerusalem. Ye are witnesses of these things." [6] There can be no better description of what the counsel of God is than that which is contained in these words; and this counsel, as so defined and set forth, forms the limit of the commission which every preacher of the word has received from his Master.

The preacher of the word is therefore pre-eminently a witness bearer. He is no mere searcher for truth, who gropes uncertainly along a blind path, as a pioneer, leading timidly and hesitatingly those who choose to follow him. He

[6] Luke xxiv. 44-48.

is no mere philosopher, who guesses at verities, and who, under the dim guidance of surmises and hypotheses, brings himself and those who adhere to him into the mist and mire of speculation. He is not a man set apart to give utterance to opinions that have no better basis than his own or others' imagination. He is on the contrary simply an ambassador, with a well defined and clearly revealed message to deliver from God to man—a message having but one central theme and one definite aim; that theme being the Saviour of our humanity, and that aim the salvation of men—an aim achieved first, by leading men to Christ, and then, by building them up on this foundation. And everything that does not directly or indirectly bear upon this theme, and that does not directly or indirectly further this aim, is extraneous to his commission, and outwith the limits of his office.

This is a view which, I think, we have special need to keep before our minds in the present day. For there are tendencies which would make the gospel ministry a kind of service with a roving commission to discant on anything and everything under the sun; tendencies which would degrade the pulpit to the level of a platform for the discussion of merely mundane questions—for the thrashing out of current topics, for discoursing on matters of history, philosophy, science, art, literature, politics, society scandals, and a host of other things, which the most vivid imagination and the widest charity cannot, by any means, connect with man's highest welfare and eternal destiny. True indeed it is, that everything human has, and is bound to have, a more or less appreciable effect upon man as a spiritual and an immortal being, but here the *less* is so much more evident than the *more*, that he who tries to reach the soul, for the saving and the sanctifying of it, by such means is like a man who, wishing to go from one end of the town to the other should, instead of taking the direct road, go round the entire world in order to reach his destination. Thus it is when the preacher of the word forgets his sacred commission and panders to the multitude, which, impatient of spiritual truth, would fain make the service of God in the sanctuary rather an entertainment than an act of worship and a means of grace. If we would guard our highest interests, and preserve from sacrilege that which is most sacred amongst us, we must resist every profaning tendency that would change the house of God and the place of prayer into a mere lecture hall or an arena for the discussion of temporal affairs.

I have said that "the counsel of God" forms the limits of the preacher's commission; but, when I use the word *limits*, I do not wish you to infer that the range or scope of one who confines himself therein is by any means narrow or inconsiderable. "The counsel of God" is set forth in the word of God, and there is no lack of space and of variety within the sacred oracles. None need feel under special restraint who has the whole of Revelation to traverse, and who may wander where he will in all its length and breadth, when seeking to know and declare the mind of God. It is by no means necessary to go forth from the circle of those sacred Scriptures that testify of Christ, in order to behold Him, and the truth regarding Him, and regarding His work for, and His purpose relative to our humanity, in fresh aspects; for, however much we may have studied these divine writings in the past, and, however far and wide may have been our excursions through them, there ever remains far more to be apprehended than we yet know, and an infinitely greater diversity of view from which truth may be seen than we have yet occupied. And withal there are themes within the inspired record far more entrancing, far more worthy of our attention, as well as unspeakably more valuable for us as immortal creatures than aught we can find beyond it. For the book which the commission of the preacher of the word warrants him to use, as the basis of his message to men, is the Book of the universe—not a narrow, sectional, and merely earthly Book, but one by which he may mount up to heaven, and tell of the throne of the eternal; [7] descend to the depths, and warn of "the blackness of darkness for ever"; [8] revel in the mysteries of divine plan and purpose relative to man's redemption, beholding verities which even "the angels desire to look into"; [9] wing his way to east or west without limit, to find all under the power of God and peopled by His "ministering spirits"; [10] pierce backward to the beginning of time and stand with the Creator on the threshold of human history, [11] or travel in faith forward to that consummation when "time shall be no longer," [12] and gaze there on things which "eye hath not seen, nor ear heard, neither have entered into the heart of man." [13] Truly it is only in accommodation to our weakness of apprehension that we speak of "limits" at all in connection with "the counsel of God," for this is infinitude, and he who has so wide, and great, and glorious a field to traverse, has no excuse for divergence to matters of infinitely less moment, and of infinitely narrower range.

[7] Ezek. i. 26 ff.   [8] Jude 13.   [9] 1 Pet. i. 12.
[10] Ps. civ. 4.   [11] Heb. i. 6, 7, 14.   [12] Rev. x. 6.   [13] 1 Cor. i. 9.

There is, however, one thing that may well be added here, and without which misapprehension might arise. Although the range of the preacher be so wide, and he may legitimately discourse on so many and so varied themes, yet there is one central Person and one central point to which he must ever be returning, and toward which all the lines of his expounding and proclaiming of truth must ever converge, and that one Person is the Lord Jesus Christ, and that one point, His death upon the Cross. As whilst the voyager or traveller explores sea and lake, river and mountain, prairie and forest in all quarters of the globe, the needle of the compass which he carries still points to the pole, so whilst the preacher leads his hearers through the length and breadth of the Word of God—that spiritual world whose features are as many and diverse as are those of the natural world—there should ever be a pointing to Christ and Him Crucified—the Pole-star of our faith, the Guide of all our wandering, and the Goal as well of all our progress. In this sense there is a limit to the preacher's commission, and that limit is, THE CROSS OF CHRIST.

But I am led by this to ask your attention now, in the second place, to *the extent of the preacher's commission*: "The *whole* counsel of God." In view of what I have just said, it is manifest that we must understand the phrase, as I have quoted it from our text, in a comparative sense. No one, not even the apostle Paul, could absolutely, within the limits of any ministry, however long, declare "the *whole* counsel of God." But what the apostle means to say is this, that, so far as time and opportunity had permitted him, he had not suppressed aught which it was his duty to proclaim as the ambassador of Christ, or, to put it in words which he makes use of in an earlier part of his address, "I shrank not from declaring unto you anything that was profitable." [14] He took no narrow view of his work as a messenger of Christ, did not confine himself to what are elsewhere called "the rudiments of the first principles," [15] but led those who waited upon his preaching into the deep things of the faith, possibly, in his verbal instructions as afterwards in his epistles, uttering some things which were "hard to be understood." [16] Now, if sometimes preachers and people take too wide a view of the scope and purpose of the pulpit, intermingling things mundane and material with things heavenly and spiritual, at other times too narrow a view is taken of the work of the ministry, and he who proclaims the truth is spoken of, as not sufficiently evangelical, because he does not confine himself to a few of the more elementary verities of the faith, but feels it to be his duty to show that the commandment of the Lord is "exceeding broad." [17] But if a man is to declare "the whole counsel of God," so far as he has apprehended it, or so far as it has been revealed to him, is he not culpable if he hide or ignore any part? Those who speak for the Lord Jesus are not entrusted only with a part of the verities of the gospel, but with the entire range thereof, and they cannot be true to themselves, or true to their Master, unless they seek to preserve some proportion, of a just and complete nature, between their utterances and their message in all its fulness. Moreover, "the whole counsel of God" is needed for man, and it is not for this one and that one to determine that a certain

---

[14] Acts xx. 20.   [15] Heb. v. 12; vi. 1.   [16] 2 Pet. iii. 16.
[17] Ps. cxix. 96.

part shall be made use of, and another part left untouched. We must not pick and choose as if we were the judges as to what would be best for us to speak or to hear. There is no part of the revealed word that has not its claims upon our attention, and that has not its use for the conversion or the sanctification of the soul. And truths have never been neglected for any length of time without the penalty being paid for their neglect by the growth of the error or errors which stand directly opposed to them. This, the history of the church, has but too surely and sadly proved, many of its most virulent and pestilential heresies having been due to unfaithfulness to certain phases of spiritual verity, or to the emphasising of one part of "the counsel of God" at the expense of another. And precisely that which arises in the history of the church, from this cause, will occur in the history of the individual life from a like cause. Mis-shapen Christians are the product of neglect of some portion of the truth which should be taught. If we see a believer narrow, illiberal, prejudiced, angular, or in some other way twisted out of the fair proportions of the perfect man in Christ Jesus, rest assured that the cause is to be found either in some defect of the preaching on which he has been fed, or on a refusal on his part to accept and assimilate "the whole counsel of God," though it has been placed before him.

But without dwelling longer on this phase of our subject I ask your attention in the last place to *the preacher's temptation*: To *shrink* from declaring "the whole counsel of God." I have never yet met the man or woman to whom the word of God in every part was palatable. No matter how much there may have been of profession to receive the whole divine word, or of sincere intention to be absolutely guided thereby, there are ever lurking reservations, or convenient explanations, that indicate the hidden dislike of the heart, and the secret, though unexpressed wish that "the counsel of God" were otherwise. Hence it sometimes happens that certain themes of the preacher are displeasing; and, if one be afraid or unwilling to incur disfavour, there results a shrinking from the presentation of such themes, and a tendency to slur them over. Now I need not say that this is unfaithfulness both to man and to God. It is unfaithfulness to man; for it is invariably the case, that those phases of truth that are least welcome to us are those phases of which we stand most in need. It is just because they are corrective that they are displeasing; just because they ruffle some feeling of content with a condition of things that should not exist in our lives, that we do not care for them; just because they interfere with some pleasure or pursuit which is dear to us, that we would fain not have them. But on the other hand for these very reasons—that is because they are corrective, because they disturb a false content, because they interfere with an unholy pleasure or an evil pursuit, there is special need that they be presented and urged upon us. And, accordingly, to refrain from doing so, on account of their unpalatableness, is for the preacher to act an unfaithful part towards those to whom he ministers. It is not to be expected that his message should always be well-pleasing. This might be so, if those to whom he ministers were perfect creatures—though in such case they would have no need of his ministrations—but it cannot be so, so long as his ministry is a ministry to sinful men. For just as medicines for the body are not over well-pleasing to take, so medicines for the soul cannot be always honied. We must expect the sharp and the bitter, and we should not complain of occasional pungency. It is, I apprehend, the worst of all signs when the words of the preacher are ever in your ears "as a very lovely song of one that hath a pleasant voice, and can play well on an instrument."[18] Rest assured that you will, in that case, find but little to profit, and more to lull you into spiritual sleep than to quicken you into high and healthful life.

I need not, I am sure, enter into detail in order to show that whoso preaches the word and shrinks from declaring "the whole counsel of God" is not only unfaithful to man, but as well unfaithful to God. For it is plain, that if one is appointed to perform a duty, and only performs part thereof, he lacks in fidelity in proportion as his work lacks in completeness. And this is just the case with such as, having been commissioned by the divine Master to bear His message to men, fail in the full delivery thereof; they prove themselves wanting in an essential of their office, and they hinder, by their failure, the full and the free development of the Saviour's cause. For what they are set apart to do is to declare the truth, the whole truth, and nothing but the truth; let them speak that which is false, or hide that which is true, or go beyond that which is revealed, and they incur blame, and involve themselves in the grave charge of being untrue to Him Whose they are and Whom they profess to serve.

It should therefore be the aim both of preacher and of people so to speak, and so to hear, that neither on the one side, nor on the other, shall there be any shrinking from declaring or receiving "the whole counsel of God." In this

[18] Ezek. xxxiii. 32.

respect they may indeed be mutually helpful, the one by rising superior to the prejudices and the narrowness of his own heart, and of the hearts of those amidst whom he is placed; and the other by freely welcoming every word of exhortation, or warning, or instruction, for which appeal may be made to the law and to the testimony. Let the one aim at pleasing God and not men, and the other desire rather that which is profitable than that which is pleasing, and there shall be little fear of any part of the divine mind, essential to man's well-being, being left without expression and without reception: the one shall not fail in proclaiming, and the other not fail in accepting "the whole counsel of God."

It may seem to some of you that the theme which has been occupying our attention this forenoon is one rather fitted for preachers than for hearers, and that its counsels and warnings are more appropriate to myself than to you. And perhaps this is so; but I am sure you will excuse the apparent inaptness of the subject, when I tell you that I have been led to choose it specially by the fact that it is this day—even I might say to the very hour—exactly twenty-one years since I was ordained over this congregation as its minister. And, if now I preach a sermon that has more fitness for myself than for you, it is that I may realise the more vividly that ideal which every Christian minister should keep before him, and endeavour to reach. I would not venture to say, with confidence, this day that I have not shrank from declaring unto you "the whole counsel of God," but this I will say, without egotism, that I am not conscious of having ever avoided the enunciation of what I believed to be true during the course of these twenty-one years in which I have ministered in your midst. I have at least *tried* to declare to you "the whole counsel of God," and I say *this*, even though it may be that, on account of my own limitations, I may have failed to do so. I have never been deterred in my preaching by the fear of any one, and I have never been guided in it by the desire to gain the favour of any one. And let me say that, to do you justice as a congregation, there has never been to my knowledge, directly or indirectly, any attempt or any desire on your part to interfere with me in the delivery of the message with which I have regarded myself as charged. So far as you are concerned I have had absolute freedom to set forth "the whole counsel of God." And I believe I have profited by this liberty—a liberty which every preacher must lay claim to, for to his own Master he stands or falls. [19]

And now, looking back, I feel impelled to ask, What is the product of these years of a faithful endeavour to preach the truth? This is a question which I am by no means able to answer. And yet there have not been lacking indications of such success as a minister most desires. Not a few have confessed that they have been led to the Lord Jesus, others have acknowledged spiritual benefit which has helped them on the way of Christian life, and many who have now passed away from our midst have testified that they were being made strong for their last journey by the verities which it has been my privilege to preach. I can also say that the manifestations of Christian activity in our midst, the development of a deeper sense of responsibility relative to those who are living around us in a state of unbelief, contrasts favourably with that which obtained in past years, and I trust may be reckoned as a sign

[19] Rom, xiv. 4.

that the declaration of "the counsel of God" has not been fruitless. But what I wish most to emphasise to-day, both for my own benefit and yours, is the responsibility associated with lengthened preaching and lengthened hearing of the word of God. There can be no satisfaction in having spoken so long for the Master unless there has been an earnest endeavour to be faithful to the trust entailed; such an endeavour that one is able to say, as said the apostle, "I testify unto you this day, that I am pure from the blood of all men." And again, on the other hand, there can be no satisfaction in listening so long to the word spoken in behalf of the Master unless there has been an earnest endeavour to give heed to that word, and a faithful attempt to carry out its behests. These considerations I would urge to-day upon myself and upon you, that, in the future, I may be the more faithful in preaching, and you the more faithful in hearing. For this is the twofold lesson that is brought home to our minds, and that may, I trust, be profoundly impressed upon our hearts.

A minister of the word is "a dying man speaking to dying men."[20] This fact is often borne in upon my soul as I stand here and utter the message of the gospel. Of that congregation that sat in these pews when, twenty-one years ago, I preached my first sermon, as your minister, more than the half have "fallen asleep." The number of those in their graves is greater than the number of those who remain. Does not this fact—which is no unique or exceptional thing, but is only the average of mortality—bring home to us, very pointedly,

---

[20] " I preached as never sure to preach again
      And as a dying man to dying men."
                    —Richard Baxter, *Love breathing Thanks and Praise.*

the need for the faithful preaching and the faithful hearing of "the whole counsel of God?" We too are hastening onward; how long or how short we may be together no one can venture to predict. Let us therefore seek to perform our respective duties as minister and as people that, whenever we may part, it may be in the sure hope of meeting again, and of receiving the Master's commendation. "And now, brethren, I commend you to God, and to the word of His grace, which is able to build you up and to give you an inheritance among all them that are sanctified."[21] May the great Shepherd of the sheep keep your souls and mine in perfect safety until the day of His appearing, and when He is manifested may it be our mutual lot to receive an abundant entrance into the inheritance of the saints in light and crowns of glory that shall not fade away.

[21] Acts. xx. 32.

APPENDIX.

Then opened He their mind, that they might understand the Scriptures; and He said unto them, Thus it is written, that the Christ should suffer, and rise again from the dead the third day; and that repentance and remission of sins should be preached in His name.
—LUKE XXIV. 45-47.

The Holy Spirit, whom the Father will send in My name, He shall teach you all things and bring to your remembrance all that I said unto you . . . He shall bear witness of Me, and ye also bear witness.
—JOHN XIV. 26; XV. 26, 27.

We have the mind of Christ.
—PAUL : I. CORINTHIANS II. 16.

APPENDIX.

THE MIND OF CHRIST.

There are some, in the present day, who seem particularly anxious to institute a quarrel between our Lord and His apostles, and especially between Christ and Paul. The form which their endeavour takes is to assume that the teaching of Jesus has been misunderstood and misrepresented by those of His followers whose writings are to be found in the Epistles and in the book of Revelation. Setting aside the plain intimation and promise which the Master gave to His disciples, that, for the guidance of them in the fulfilment of their duty as His witness-bearers to the world, He would send them a special gift of the Holy Spirit, Who would teach them all things, and bring all things to their remembrance, whatsoever He had said,[1] these critics pretend to discover discrepancies and inconsistencies between the doctrine of Christ and the doctrine which His apostles set forth. And they are for ever saying, "Back to Christ, get at what He Himself taught, not as it appears coloured by passing through the mind of Paul or James or Peter or John." Now the very fact that this is said proceeds upon the assumption that these cannot, or at least do not, represent the mind of Christ; that we have in them a gloss upon His more pure and perfect teaching, and that we must to a certain degree discount the representations which they make of the gospel, and especially of the nature of the work of Christ upon which the gospel is founded.

That we may be helped to the entertainment of just views on this important matter I ask attention, in the first place, to the question as to *how the mind of Christ has been expressed*. Primarily, of course, it is set forth in His own words and deeds, for in seeking to get at it we must have respect not only to what He said, but as well, and that with equal attention, to what He did. There are those who would find in His language alone the exhibition of His thought. They emphasise His discourses, and, in particular, that inaugural

[1] John xiv. 26.

word which He spoke as the proclamation, and, in part, the description of the laws and privileges of His kingdom—the Sermon on the mount. Now, the words of the Lord Jesus are of inestimable value, we cannot measure their worth, we cannot utter regarding them estimates that are exaggerated—they are the wisest, the noblest, the highest, the purest words ever uttered by human lips, "Never man spake like this Man." [2] But we shall wrong our Lord if we insist upon the principle that His mind was only expressed in His words. We shall cut ourselves off from more than the half of His teaching, shall shut our eyes and ears to a great and most important part of His doctrine. As a matter of fact, when we seek to get at the mind of any of our fellow men, we are not satisfied with merely knowing what they have said in so many words. The limitations of language make speech, even at the best, but an imperfect mirror of thought. And especially when it is our desire to have revealed to us the inner disposition, spirit, motives, tendencies, purposes, and plans of an individual—in short the mind of the individual in the widest sense, we do not confine our observation to his words alone, we seek to know his acts, nay, we actually set more store upon these than upon that which he may say, we recognise in them a more complete and satisfactory exhibition of what he means, and of what he would have us understand regarding himself, than the most copious explanations which he can give us by word of mouth. Now this common-sense method, which we are constantly employing in seeking to get at the mind of our fellow-men, must by no means be discarded when we seek to get at the mind of Christ. It is impossible too strongly to protest against the entirely partial and one-sided means which have been of late so widely adopted, in seeking to discover the inner thought and plan of Christ's mission, by the exaltation of His speech, as if it were the only factor available for this end, and the utter neglect of what is of equal if not more importance His doing and His suffering. He who endeavours to find the mind of Christ, and yet does not take into his calculation the manner of our Saviour's living, and, what is of supreme moment, the fact and the manner of His dying, is most certainly taking a course that cannot but defeat the object he has in view. The mind of Christ cannot be known by any one who will not follow Him on the pathway of suffering and go with Him even as far as Golgotha. They are ignorant, and, in so far as the centre and essence of the matter is concerned, wholly ignorant, of the mind of Christ who

[2] John vii. 46.

have not seen Him on the Cross. They cannot learn that mind in its deepest meaning if they have not learned it at Calvary. This He Himself has declared in these words "Whosoever doth not bear his own cross and come after Me, cannot be My disciple;"[3] that is, if any man would be a disciple of Mine, a learner at My feet; if any man would know My mind—he must "take up his cross and follow Me."[4] And follow Christ where? Where save to the place of cross-bearing? There, as nowhere else, you shall be in a position to get at His mind, to understand Him, and to obtain such insight and inspiration that ultimately—for this is the aim and end of all such learning—His mind shall be in you. For there indeed you shall find the key that will open up and interpret for you many of His most precious and gracious words and works.

But in considering how the mind of Christ has been expressed, it is by no means enough to have regard to what He Himself said and did. For such a course assumes that within the limits of the gospel narratives we have all the elements necessary for the formation of perfect conclusions as to the entire purpose, character, and issue of Christ's kingdom, as these lay wrapped up in His own thought. Now we have the most convincing evidence that this is an erroneous assumption. The personal teaching of the Lord Jesus was professedly incomplete; and the facts of His doing and suffering were, as to their inner meaning, left for future revelation. To His apostles He declared "I have yet many things to say unto you, but ye cannot bear them now."[5] In the prediction of the Holy Spirit, which immediately follows this statement, there was definitely promised further instruction as to His mind and will. "Howbeit when He, the Spirit of truth, is come, He shall guide you into all truth, for He shall not speak from Himself; but what things soever He shall hear, these shall He speak; and He shall declare unto you the things that are to come. He shall glorify Me: for He shall take of Mine and shall declare it unto you."[6] Succeeding the day of Pentecost there are immediate evidences presented of a fuller and more exact apprehension of the design of His death than we find to have prevailed amongst the disciples during the period of His ministry; and these evidences are in harmony with His own predictions as to the work which His Holy Spirit was to perform—the work of illumination, the work of more perfectly revealing His mind, and thereby making His apostles more fit to be witness-bearers

[3] Luke xiv. 27. [4] Mat. xvi. 24. [5] John xvi. 12.
[6] Ibid v. 13, 14. See also John xiv. 16, 17, 26; xv. 26; xvi. 7-11.

thereof. [7] And in view of these and other considerations that might be added, were we to go fully into the matter, it is manifest that when we endeavour to find the mind of Christ we must, by no means, confine ourselves to the records of the gospels. Through the inspiration of the divine Spirit the writings of the apostles have been made transparencies, which show forth, with the utmost clearness, and, in its legitimate development, the thought of the Lord Jesus. It is no vain boast which Paul makes when he declares " We have the mind of Christ." [8] It is a simple statement of fact which, as we have seen, harmonises with that which our Lord Himself in His parting addresses to His disciples led them and us to expect. These disciples truly speak to us, in their epistles, not only in the name, but, we might almost say, in the very words of the Lord Jesus. They stand to us in this respect " in Christ's stead," [9] and we dare not, save at the risk of most serious misapprehension and incompleteness, disregard the testimony which they afford. He who has the mind of Christ, after the fashion in which Paul and the other writers of the New Testament profess to have it, will not misunderstand and misrepresent the meaning of the Master. And hence we may well suspect and regard with disfavour any attempt to set against each other, as if they were opposed and inconsistent, the apostolic writings and the sayings of the Lord Jesus. To neglect the one on pretence of paying greater heed to the other, is in truth, to doubt and question the provision which Christ Himself made for the promulgation of His word and the establishment of His kingdom.

But having now sought to realise how the mind of Christ has been expressed, I remark further, that *the mind of Christ is the heritage of the church.* There is a sense in which all disciples of the Lord can make use of the words which Paul employs. A treasure has been laid up in store for them, which avails for every age, and is of the utmost moment for every believer. Our Saviour has not only by word and deed, by personal teaching through language and act and by means of His inspired followers made known His mind, but He has as well secured its transmission to subsequent generations of His people. It has not been left to float down on the uncertain current of tradition, it has not been committed to the charge of those who might be unequal to the task of its preservation

---

[7] Compare and contrast the language of Peter in his sermon on the day of Pentecost with his language before the descent of the Holy Spirit, especially setting over against each other, Acts ii. 23, 36, 38 and Mat. xvi. 22. See also 1 Pet. i. 18, 19; 1 John i. 7. ii. 2, as indicating the advance of these apostles in the apprehension of the mind of Christ.   [8] 1 Cor. ii. 16.   [9] 2 Cor. v. 20.

or its repetition ; on the contrary, it is embedded in those sacred Scriptures which have been "inspired of God," [10] and set forth by holy men who spoke and wrote as they were moved by the Holy Ghost. This is just what we would expect in view of its importance, and in view of the necessity of so sending the record of it down to the ages that those for whom it is designed might have confidence in it as a real, an accurate, and a sufficient representation of the doctrine of the Lord Jesus. And it is because we have possession of this that there is a sense, and a very genuine sense, in which every disciple can join in the affirmation "We have the mind of Christ." This is a heritage which has been by special means secured to us. And we are justified in saying that it is as certainly ours as it was their's to whom it was first given. The lapse of time has not placed us at any disadvantage in respect of this. Although we are remote from the period of the personal ministry of our Lord, we may assert that we have as perfect means of knowing what His mind is as had those who listened to His voice, or to the voices of the messengers who were sent forth in His name. And when we take into account the saying, the doing, and the suffering of our Lord, and along with these the speech and the writing of those whom He inspired, there can be little doubt that the supreme expression of His mind finds its most fitting symbol, and that to which it is chiefly designed to draw the eyes of sinful humanity in what has been the object of our study—THE CROSS OF CHRIST.

[10] 2 Tim. iii. 16.

THE END.

www.ingramcontent.com/pod-product-compliance
Lightning Source LLC
Chambersburg PA
CBHW021815230426
43669CB00008B/761